KEYBOARD PROFICIENCY

LOUISE GUHL

Emeritus, University of Minnesota

D0573305

DORSET PRESS

New York

To the memory of my husband
Franz

And for my friend
Gwen

Copyright © Louise Guhl, 1979

All rights reserved. No part of this publication may be reproduced or transmitted in any form or by any means, electronic or mechanical, including photocopy, recording, or any information storage and retrieval system, without permission in writing from the publisher.

This edition published by Dorset Press, a division of Marboro Books Corporation, by arrangement with Louise Guhl.

1987 Dorset Press

ISBN 0-88029-130-3

Library of Congress Catalog Card Number: 78-70796

Text and music composition by Music-Book Associates, Inc., New York, N.Y.

Acknowledgments
Photographs on pp. 2, 3, and 35 by Dwight Barnes Studio. Latvian melodies on pp. 50, 51, 52, 53, 55, 108, and 173 are from four study books, *Latvian Melodies for the Piano,* assembled by Guna Kalmite-Skujina, and are reprinted with her permission.

Printed in the United States of America

M 9 8 7 6 5 4

PREFACE

Keyboard Proficiency, a text for the basic class-piano course, is intended for the college music major who performs as a singer or on an instrument other than the keyboard but has had no piano instruction. It is also useful for the high school student planning to major in music, and it provides effective material for the student who has had piano lessons and wants to improve the functional skills of reading, playing by ear, transposing, harmonizing, and improvising.

The book is intended for class instruction and contains material for one academic year; an outline of how it might be used follows. It is also suitable for individual instruction. The approach and materials were developed while the author was on the staff of the Department of Music, University of Minnesota, and they draw upon long experience in teaching and observing the learning process in students of all ages, from four years old through the graduate level.

Reading music for two hands at once is usually very difficult for performers accustomed to music scored on one staff in only one clef. This text mitigates the problem by approaching piano playing as a sensorimotor skill—that is, one in which the arms, hands, and fingers move in response to a stimulus, the keyboard. The reading material in the text is ordered so that the student uses brain, eyes, ears, and sense of pulse to direct the required muscles to play in time.

In each of the eight units, the various activities are correlated to a specific level of competence. Unit One introduces the technical foundation for physical ease at the keyboard and begins the reading process. The subsequent units develop technique and reading while dealing with the other functional skills.

Reading and harmonizing in keys with more than one or two sharps or flats is another difficult task for students. All keys are included in the book, but they are presented in a manner that gives the student time both to gain a clear mental image of the piano keys in each tonality and to develop swift recall of those keys while reading, harmonizing, and transposing. Thus the activities in Units Two through Four concentrate first on the pentachord patterns that lie within the normal five-finger hand span, then on fingering over an expanded range, with changing hand positions. Units Five and Six deal with key signatures of not more than two sharps or flats, through activities designed to teach the scales of these tonalities as well as the theory needed for harmonizing and improvising with them. Unit Seven consists entirely of sight reading and repertoire in those keys. The remaining key signatures, with pertinent fingering patterns, are supplied in Unit Eight.

While the primary focus of the book is on playing in major and minor, material on the five other commonly used modes appears in compact sections throughout the text. This material is intended to be used as the instructor thinks best; it is useful for a broader understanding, since students frequently associate a given key signature with only its major and minor tonalities. The texture of piano music makes concrete the existence of other modalities probably more readily than does a single melodic line played by another instrument.

The music for sight reading and repertoire is an important part of the teaching approach in this book. Because the quickest way for a student to learn to play in time is to play along with someone who will not falter, the sight-reading selections are intended for the class to play ensemble. A piece should be played ensemble the very first time it is read, either by the class, or by the instructor and class together, using the headphones so that each student hears himself playing with the instructor. For developing skill it is the very first reading of a score that is most effective; hence there must be much ensemble reading of music seen for the first time. Repertoire for performance, which is too difficult to be sight-read in this way, is included throughout Units Two through Eight. The more difficult selections from Unit Five on will meet the needs of students who have had previous playing experience.

The period of time required for covering each unit will vary with the capabilities of the students and the amount of class time available. If classes meet twice weekly in an academic year divided into three quarters of ten weeks each, the following guideline should be applicable.

First quarter: Units One to Four.

Second quarter: Units Five to Seven. Unit Seven should be used concurrently with Units Five and Six, since it contains sight reading and repertoire in the same keys as the improvisation, harmonization, transposition, technique, and ear playing of Units Five and Six.

Third quarter: Unit Eight. Because most students find it harder to play in the keys presented in this unit, they will need more practice time, and they will probably not need, or be able to master, so much material at this level.

I wish to express my gratitude to Dr. Roy Schuessler, chairman of the Music Department at the University of Minnesota, who gave such unstinting support to my work in class piano and piano pedagogy; to Gwendolyn Cline Perun of the MacPhail Center for the Arts in Minneapolis, who tried out many of the devices in the book; and to all my students, who have taught me so much about learning. Among those who commented on the manuscript during its development are Madelene Zachary, University of Arkansas; Marjorie Oldfield, University of Southern California; Lawrence Rast, Northern Illinois University; Alice M. Kern, University of Michigan; Herbert Rogers, Hunter College; Ronald E. Regal, Ithaca College; Frances Larimer, Northwestern University; Nancy J. Stephenson, University of Houston; and Elyse Mach Peirick, Northeastern Illinois University. To Nina Gunzenhauser of Harcourt Brace Jovanovich goes a special tribute because of her patience while new ground was being broken, after she encouraged me to put on paper what was being done in class.

Louise Guhl

CONTENTS

UNIT ONE

Reading Piano Music

The Keyboard

The seven letters of the musical alphabet, A through G, are used to name all the white keys on the piano.

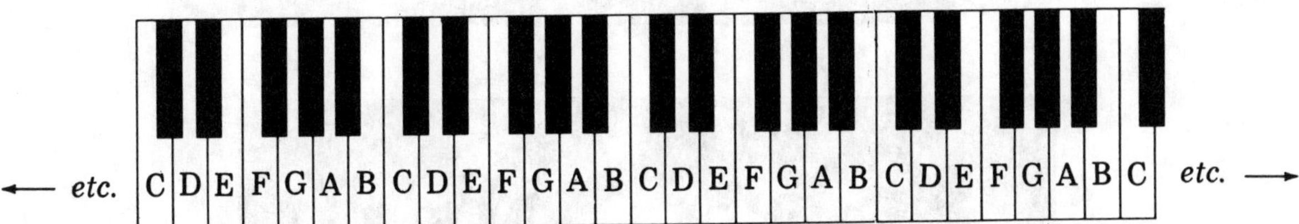

The black keys take their names from the adjacent white keys, as shown below. Thus, each black key has two names; the black key between F and G, for example, may be called either F♯ or G♭. Since there is no black key between B and C or between E and F, each of the keys in these two pairs can take the name of its adjacent key.

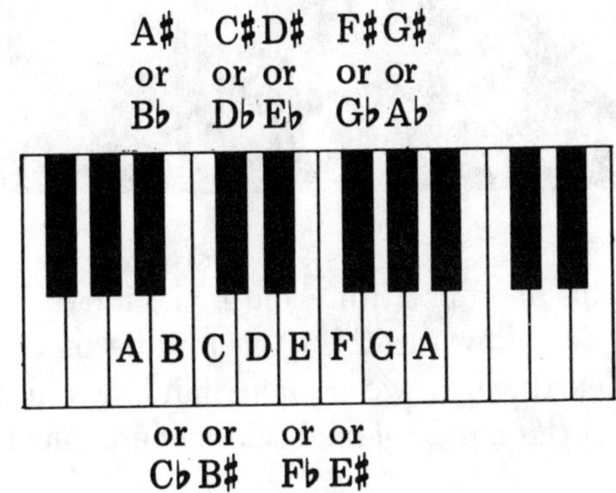

Exercise for Hand Position

1. For a comfortably arched hand position, first locate the proper key-contact points in the fingertips. Place your hands as shown in the photographs below and press your fingertips together. (Your nails should be short, as in the photographs.) The tactile sensation locates the spot where your fingers should touch the keys. Note that the little finger has less curvature than the others, and that the thumb contact point is at the corner of the nail.

2. Maintaining this hand position, center the index finger of your left hand on the C below the C in the middle of the keyboard, and place the index finger of your right hand two octaves higher. The aim is to keep the hand relaxed while energizing the index fingers

just enough to push the two C's down. Then let the fingers "ride" the keys back up, never losing key contact.

The nonplaying fingers need not be centered on specific keys if doing so produces tension in the hand. In the photograph below, note that the relaxed fingers are closer together than the key width.

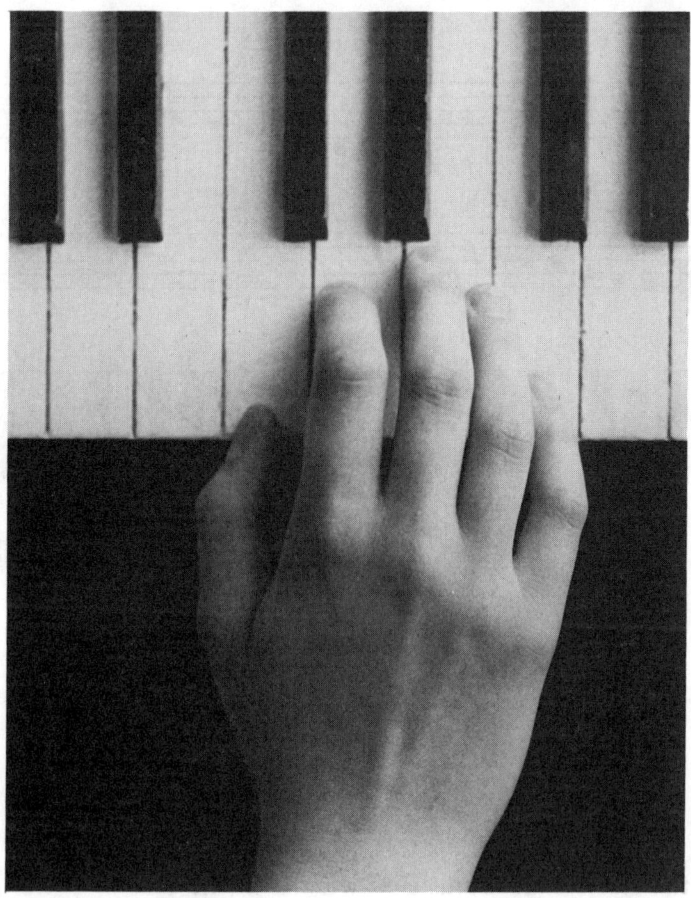

3. Now center the index finger of the left hand on middle C. Play and release C. Slide the hand downward to F, keeping it relaxed with all fingers in key contact. Play F. Slide down to the next C. Continue playing C's and F's to the bottom of the keyboard. Then repeat upward back to middle C.
4. Repeat this exercise with the right hand, playing C's and F's from middle C to the top of the keyboard and back.

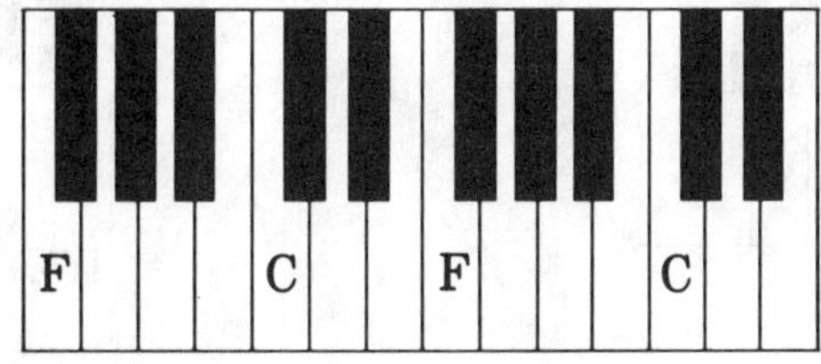

The Grand Staff

Music to be played on keyboard instruments is notated on the grand staff. Notes on the lower staff are normally played by the left hand, on the upper staff by the right hand.

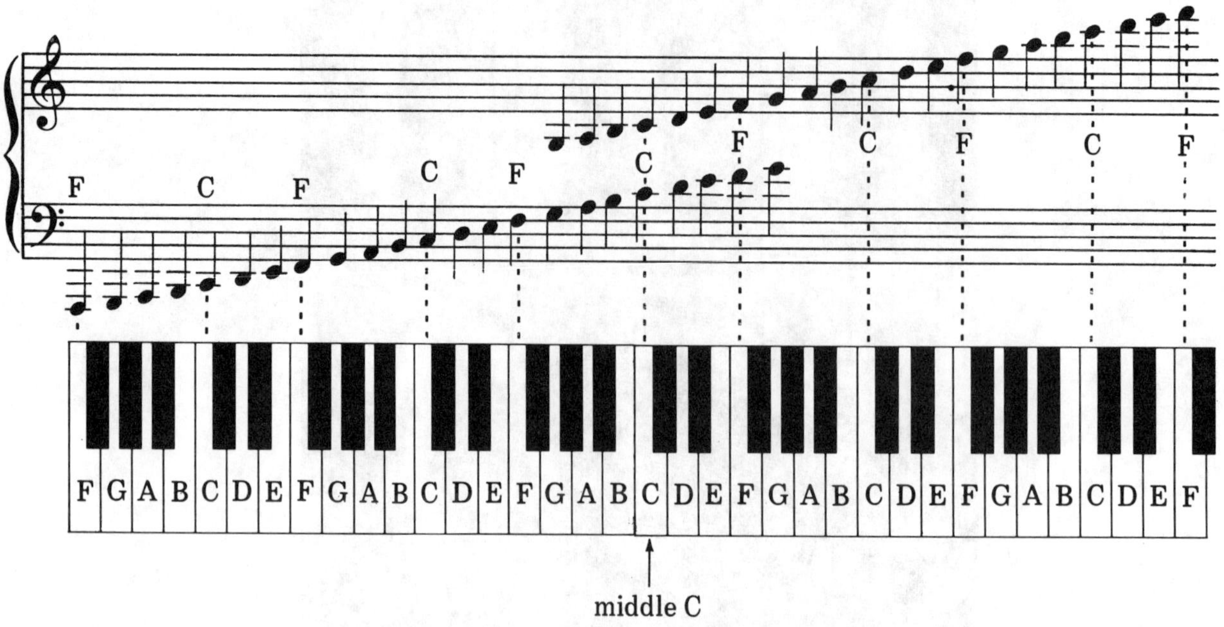

Notes on the lower staff are usually written in the bass or F clef. The clef sign indicates the location of F below middle C on the keyboard.

Notes on the upper staff are usually written in the treble or G clef, and this clef sign indicates the location of G above middle C on the keyboard.

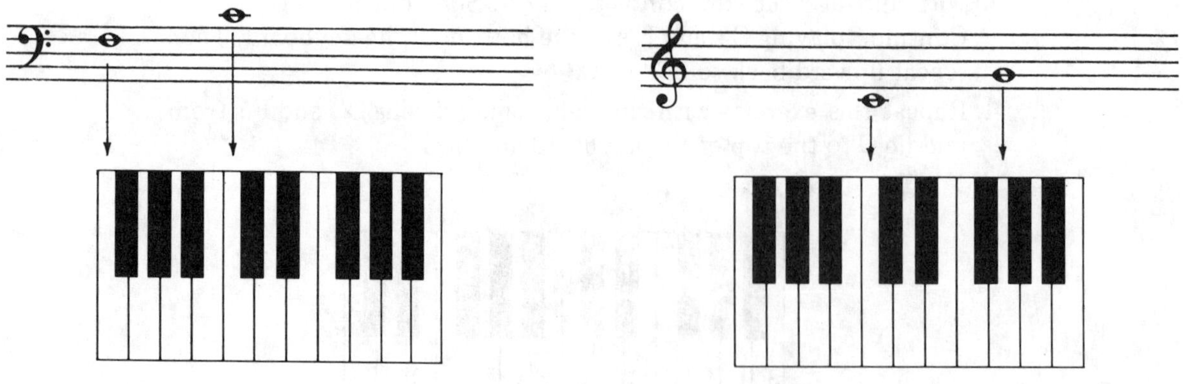

Finger Numbers

The fingers are numbered 1, 2, 3, 4, 5, starting with the thumb of each hand.

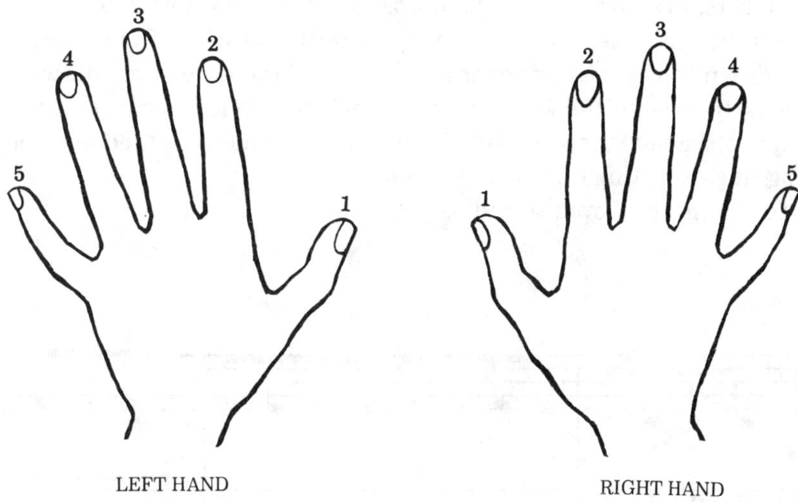

The normal hand span is five white keys wide.

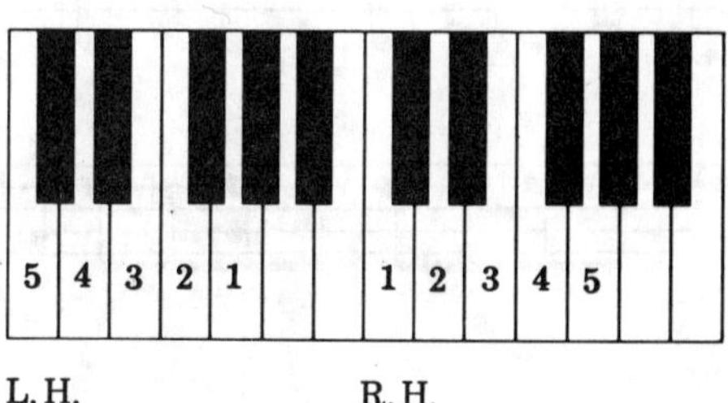

In printed piano music, fingering is indicated by small numbers placed above or below the notes. When the keys to be played lie within the hand span, only the first note is given a finger number. Succeeding notes are fingered *intervallically*—that is, adjacent keys are played with adjacent fingers and, in skips, as many fingers are skipped as keys. Intervallic fingering is shown below by the numbers in parentheses.

TECHNIQUE

Playing in Contrary Motion

The easiest way to play hands-together is in contrary motion, with matching fingers, as shown by the hand position notated on page 5.

Play the following exercise *legato* (very smoothly) by keeping the playing fingers down to the keybed for the full value of the note, then allowing those fingers to release the keys and ride back to the key surface at the exact moment the next fingers play. Try to keep the hand relaxed and the nonplaying fingers resting on the key surface.

Listen for connected, even sound.

Andante

legato

Transpose the exercise to G major by placing the thumbs as indicated, and all fingers on white keys. Read from note to note by direction, up or down.

The keyboard diagram shows that the sequence of whole and half steps on the five white keys from G to D is identical to that on the white keys from C to G, and sounds the same.

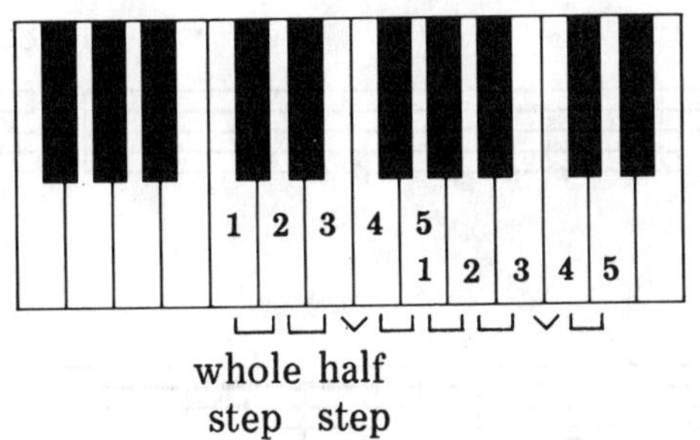

SIGHT READING

One Hand, Movement in Seconds

Use this procedure for each of the sight-reading selections that follow.

1. Start with hands resting in your lap.
2. Read the selection mentally; "hear" the pitch and rhythm mentally.
3. Scan the selection for clef, number of piano keys involved, and choice of fingers. Exercises in bass clef should be played by the left hand; those in treble clef by the right hand.
4. Identify the first note to be played by looking at the piano key for which it is the symbol.
5. Place the required fingers on the keys to be played by moving your hand directly from your lap to the specified keys. The thumb and fifth finger should rest on the key surface even when they are not playing.
6. Play legato, with relaxed hand and with the nonplaying fingers resting on the keys.
7. Aim to play the correct rhythm, pitch, and fingering the first time through.
8. At the end of the exercise, return your hand to your lap if the next exercise is for the other hand. Otherwise, leave the hand resting in position.
9. Prepare mentally for the next selection. When ready, move your hand directly into position with the proper fingers correctly placed.

7.
4
8.
2
9.
5
10.
2
3
11.
1
12.
5
13.
4
14.
5
15.
3
16.
4
17.
3
18.
2
19.
1

20.
21.
22.
23.
24.
25.
26.
27.
28.
29.

UNIT TWO
Playing with Two Hands

Rhythm for Two Hands

Much piano music is in *homophonic texture*—that is, it consists of a melody and an accompaniment. In most compositions, the right hand plays the melody, the left hand the accompaniment. Consequently, the right-hand rhythms tend to be varied, while rhythms for the left hand frequently fall into repeated patterns.

In the early stages of piano study, reading two rhythms simultaneously usually requires special attention. A rhythm you have heard is easier to play. Therefore it is helpful to voice the rhythm of the melody before playing. It is also useful, before playing, to realize the rhythm through movement.

The following exercises consist of both sound and movement. Practice each in four ways:

1. Voice the rhythm of the right-hand part with syllables, one for each note, while clapping the rhythm of the left-hand part.

2. While counting aloud, tap the rhythms with both hands, on the piano frame or your thighs. The counting should match the rhythm of the shorter notes. Thus, the example above would be counted "one and two and three and four and."
3. Tap, while counting beats only. Use a detached (*staccato*) articulation, and make a clearly audible sound: one, two, three, four.

4. Repeat the tapping without audible counting, listening closely.

(When voicing, breathe between phrases.)

1.

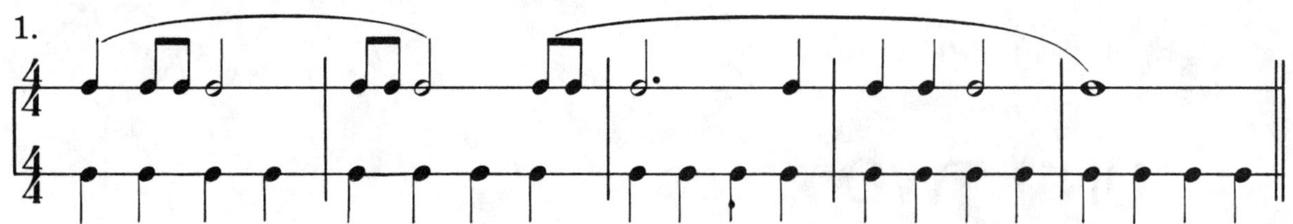

2.

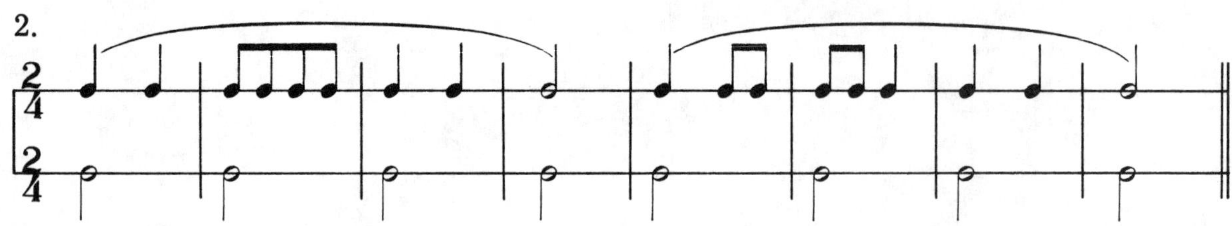

3.

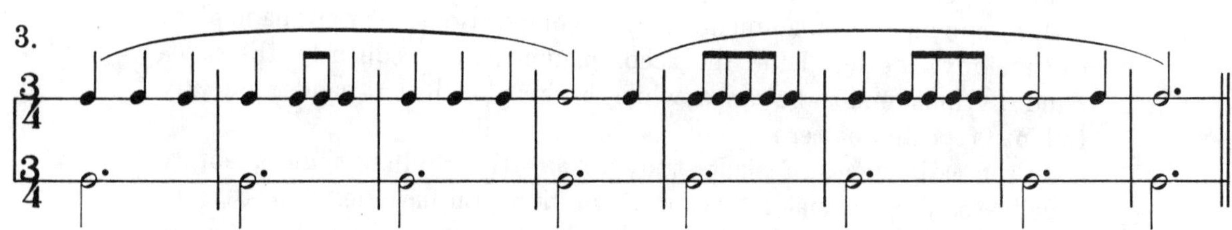

4.

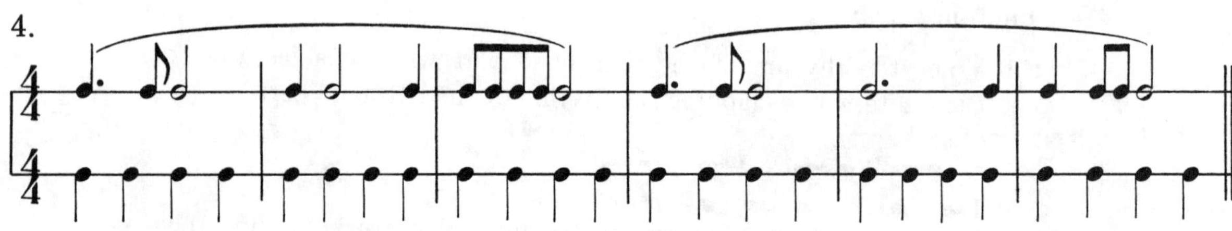

5.

6.

IMPROVISATION

Melody with Accompaniment of Perfect Fifths

1. **Structure** Rhythm and phrase structure of the six preceding exercises, pp. 12-13
L.H.: accompaniment of a perfect fifth on white keys
R.H.: melodies based on a five-finger pattern on white keys

A perfect fifth up from any white key will fall on another white key, except the fifth up from B. This fact is readily perceptible to the eye, because within the fifths C-G, D-A, and E-B lies the white-key half step from E to F; similarly, within the fifths F-C, G-D, and A-E lies the white-key half step from B to C. However, both white-key half steps lie within the fifth B-F, which is a diminished fifth, or tritone.

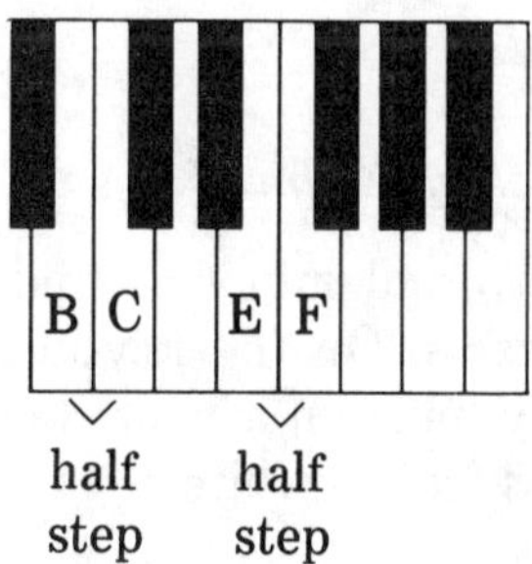

To improvise, play an accompaniment of open fifths on white keys (F and C, for example), played together with fingers 5 and 1, and create melodies playing any successive white keys desired. Keep the pitch movement predominantly in seconds (half steps or whole steps), playing skips or repeated notes where needed for a musically valid phrase, usually at or near the end of a phrase.

Develop each exercise by improvising a second section of about equal length. Play an introduction with the left hand to introduce rhythm and mood, and add a coda in the same way, if you like.

Note on improvising: It is essential to keep the beat and play in time.

2. **Structure** "A Fragment" (p. 14), measures 6-8

Sing the melody of "A Fragment" at sight, completing it by singing an improvised three-measure phrase. Repeat the improvised phrase until you can recall it easily.

Play "A Fragment" as written, hands together, aiming to reproduce exactly your improvised phrase. Once you have memorized your phrase, write it in the blank measures.

A FRAGMENT

L. G.

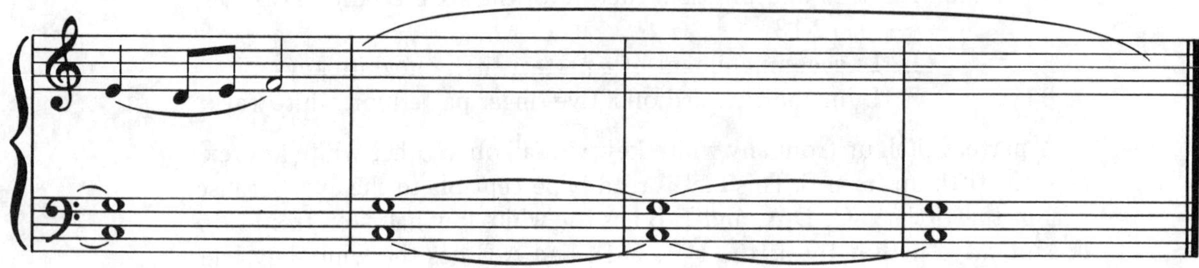

TECHNIQUE

Playing Patterns of Seconds on Black and White Keys

Major seconds (whole steps) and minor seconds (half steps) on white keys feel identical in the fingers. On the keyboard, movement in both major and minor seconds may be from a white key to a black or from a black key to a white, as well as from a white key to a white.

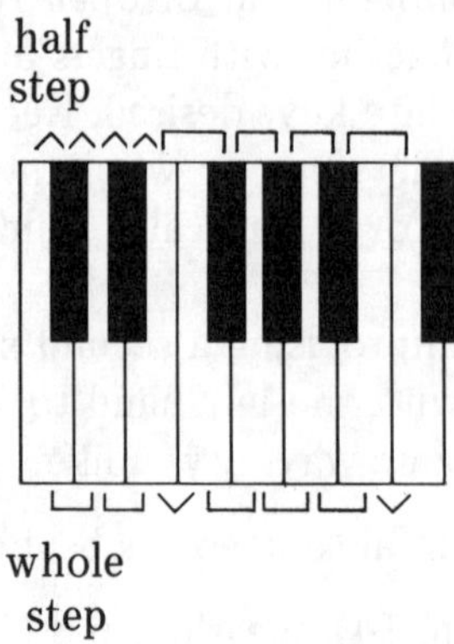

In these five exercises, place all ten fingers on the keys before playing the first note. Notice how the relative heights of your fingertips and the spaces between them vary according to the pattern of black and white keys involved.

1. Half steps: chromatic pattern

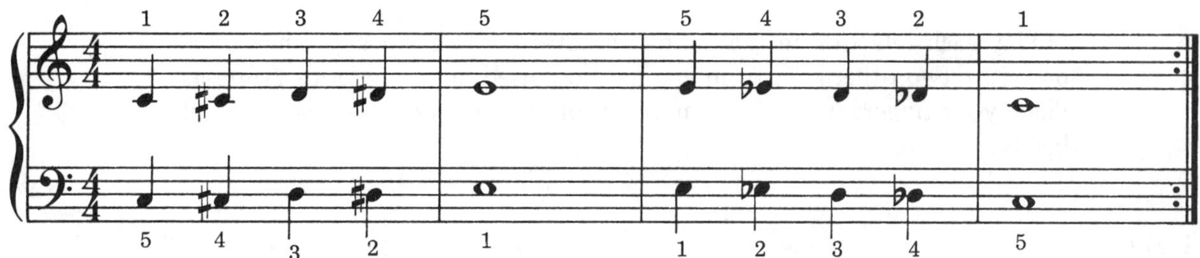

2. Whole steps: whole-tone pattern

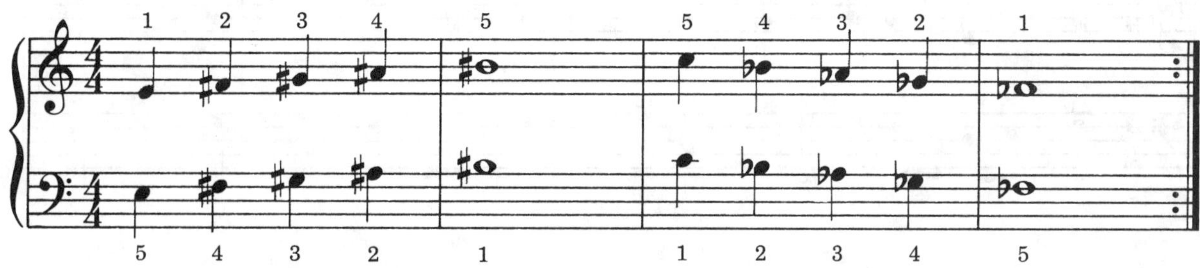

3. Major five-finger pattern: whole step, whole step, half step, whole step. Play in C, then transpose to G, D, and A major.

4. Exercise in contrary motion. Play in D, A, C, and G major.

5. Exercise in parallel motion. Play in C, G, D, and A major.

SIGHT READING

Play each selection in the hand position for the given key. Then transpose it to two other keys from among those used in the previous exercises. Place your fingers in the hand position of the new key and read intervallically.

1. D major

2. A major

3. G major

6. A major
7. D major
8. G major

TECHNIQUE

Minor Five-Finger Pattern

The minor five-finger pattern is formed by lowering the third of the major pattern a half step.

Play the following exercise in C, G, D, and A.

TRANSPOSITION

Play selections 1-8 on pages 16-18 in minor.

TECHNIQUE

Major and Minor Patterns with Only One White Key

The major and minor patterns beginning on D♭ have only one white key. They may also be notated enharmonically from C♯ as the lowest note. In common practice, the major five-note pattern is found more often notated in flats, the minor in sharps.

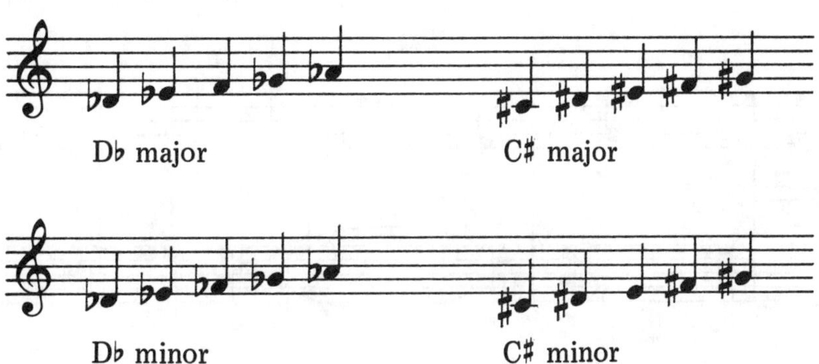

D♭ major C♯ major

D♭ minor C♯ minor

Play the following exercise with legato touch. The trill movement in measures 2-4 and 6-8 will be more comfortable if the hands tip slightly in the direction of the playing fingers.

Transpose to A♭ major and G♯ minor.

REPERTOIRE

Repertoire selections require practice for fluency and style. As a preparation for playing "Dance with Drums," sing or voice the rhythm of the melody while playing the left hand alone, before playing hands-together.

When the music calls for a fast tempo, you can save time by reading it slowly at first, and increasing the tempo gradually as performance becomes easier.

DANCE WITH DRUMS

HARMONIZATION

With Fifths on I and V

In "Dance with Drums," the harmonic basis of the accompaniment is the perfect fifth on the first degree, or tonic, of the five-note pattern on which the melody is based. (The first degree is the lowest note, commonly indicated by I in harmonic analysis.) The accompaniment of "Joshua Fought the Battle of Jericho," which is in the key of D minor, includes the perfect fifth on the fifth degree, or dominant (indicated by V).

As an accompaniment, play the perfect fifth of your choice on the first beat of each measure (indicated by an X in the score). To prepare, sing the melody, deciding by ear the choice of I or V for each measure. If you wish, sing the melody again as you play the accompaniment. Then play both the melody and accompaniment.

Note that the range of the melody includes a step below the five-note pattern, requiring a crossing of the second finger over the thumb. Such irregular fingerings are usually numbered in piano scores. Note also that a third occurs in the melody (measure 6); finger it intervallically (see p. 5).

JOSHUA FOUGHT THE BATTLE OF JERICHO

Spiritual

Transpose to G minor and A minor. (Take note of the kind of second involved in the crossover of the second finger.)

The fifth on the dominant may be inverted by playing the upper pitch an octave lower. An inverted fifth thus becomes a fourth.

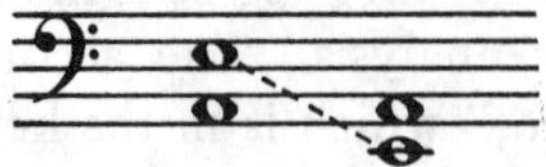

The progression from I to V may thus be played with the following voicing:

Here are two other possible accompaniment patterns for this melody.

[illegible]

Here are two other possible accompaniment patterns for this melody.

UNIT THREE
Playing All Intervals

Rhythm for Two Hands

Exercise 1 presents five basic subdivisions of the beat with the quarter note as the unit for counting. You may wish to tap each measure several times before going on to the next.

Count all the exercises in these two ways.

1. Rhythm counting: count the rhythm of all notes shorter than quarter notes, using syllables for every note.

2. Staccato beat counting: count beats only.

Tap the short notes lightly with your hand resting on your thigh or the piano frame, tapping mainly with all fingers moving up and down together. It is effective to produce a different timbre (type of sound) in each hand by tapping one hand on a wooden surface, the other on the thigh.

1.
2.
3.

4.
Introducing 3 and
5.
6.
7.

TECHNIQUE

Modality Within the Pentachord

A pentachord is a succession of five tones progressing diatonically (by seconds notated on successive staff degrees). The five-finger patterns in major and minor on pages 15 and 19 are diatonic pentachords.

Within the span of the perfect fifth, four of the modes in common usage may occur, each identifiable by the location of its half step.

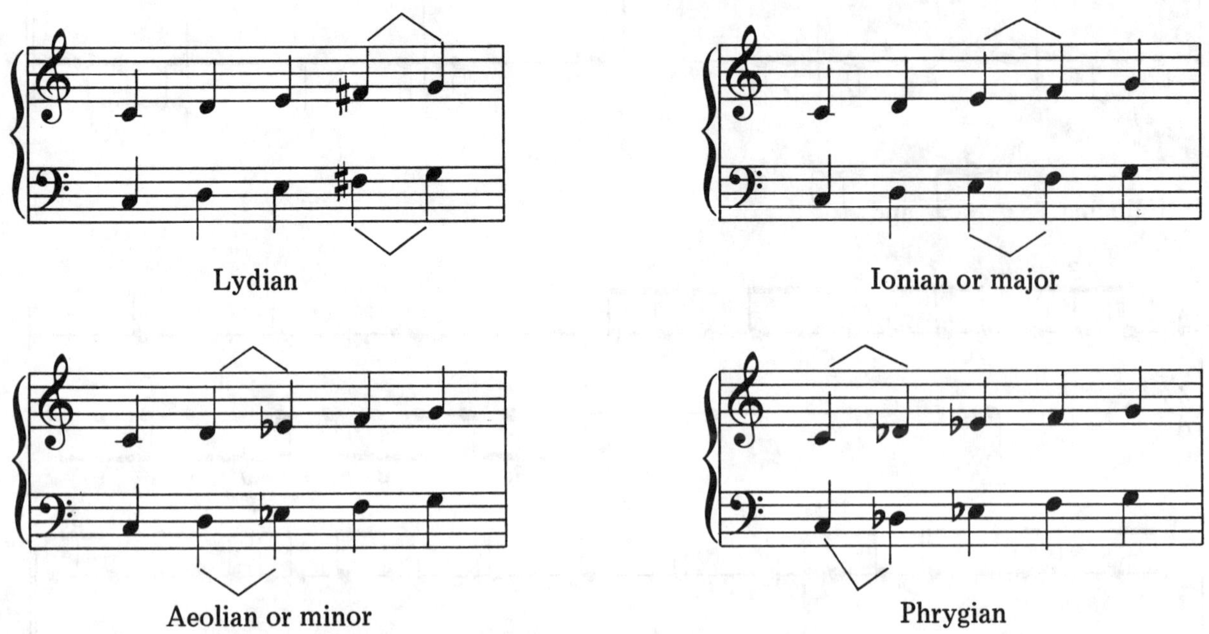

Play the following exercise in each of the modes listed above.

Transpose to modal pentachords on G, D, and A.

SIGHT READING AND TRANSPOSITION

Modal Pentachords

Before playing each of the next six exercises, scan to plan finger placement on the proper keys. Try to shape the hand correctly while it is resting in your lap. When ready, move directly to the keys for the entire position required.

Prepare by hearing the pitch and rhythm mentally.

Set a tempo by tapping out a full measure with the nonplaying hand. Continue tapping beats while playing.

When you complete each exercise, leave the playing hand in position on the keys. Prepare to transpose to a pentachord of the same structure on C, G, D, or A. Move the hand directly to the selected position, and read from note to note as if you were in the original position. It is useful to transpose each exercise to several of the pentachords.

Note that one of the pentachord positions is not diatonic.

TECHNIQUE

Intervals Within the Normal Hand Span

Within the normal hand span of a fifth lie five intervals: prime (or unison), second, third, fourth, and fifth. Unless otherwise marked in the score, the fingering for these intervals is always intervallic, as shown below.

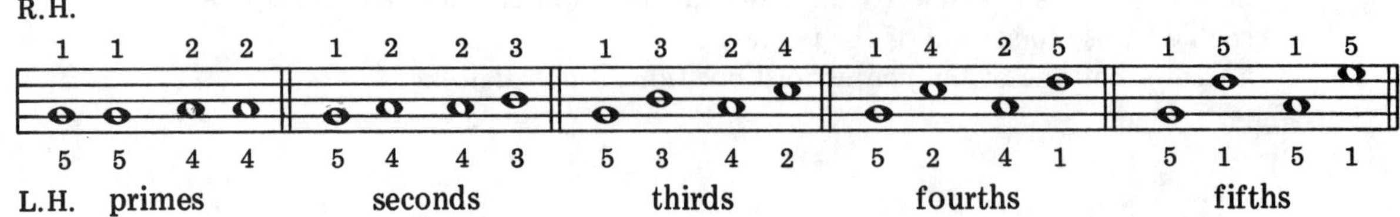

Play these two exercises in the following modal sequence: major, Lydian, again in major, minor, Phrygian.

1.

Transpose the entire sequence to G, D, A, D♭, and A♭.

2.

Transpose to G, D, A, D♭, and A♭.

SIGHT READING

One Hand, Movement in Varying Intervals

Prepare each of these six selections as suggested on page 7.

The sharps and flats to be played are omitted from the score; the hand position given indicates the correct hand placement (review pp. 28-29).

As you imagine the sound mentally before playing, choose a tempo. After playing, decide whether your choice was correct, and indicate your final choice in the blank provided.

1. Hand position: C minor

tempo ____________________

2. Hand position: G♯ Phrygian

tempo ________________

3. Hand position: D major

tempo ________________

4. Hand position: G major

tempo ________________

5. Hand position: D♭ major

tempo ________________

6. Hand position: A Lydian

TRANSPOSITION

Transpose each of the preceding sight-reading selections to a position that has the same sequence of black and white keys. For example, transpose selection 1 from C minor to G minor.

IMPROVISATION

Accompaniments for Given Melodies

Improvise accompaniments for the sight-reading selections on pages 31-33. Those in the bass clef should be played by the right hand one or two octaves higher, with the accompaniment in the left hand.

Play accompaniments of open fifths in varying rhythms suitable to the tempo of the melody. You may want to try one of the accompaniment patterns on page 23, or you may want to try one of the following suggestions.

For selections 1, 3, and 4: try fifths on I and V.

For selection 2: try fifths on I and on the second degree, which is the characteristic tone of the Phrygian mode. The fifth of F♯ is also a possibility.

For selections 5 and 6: an ostinato is a good choice for these two. (An ostinato is a short figure that repeats the same rhythm and pitch throughout a piece.) Here is a possible ostinato for selection 5:

Key Release

Well-controlled finger articulation is a necessity for clarity of sound. Thus, releasing the key must be as consciously timed as depressing the key.

Clean legato articulation results when one key is released at the *same time* another key is depressed. In printed scores, legato touch is indicated by the word *legato* or by a slur over a group of notes.

For detached articulation, one key must be released *before* the next key is depressed. Detached touch is indicated in several situations.

1. Before a rest: the key is kept depressed for the full duration of the time value of the note.

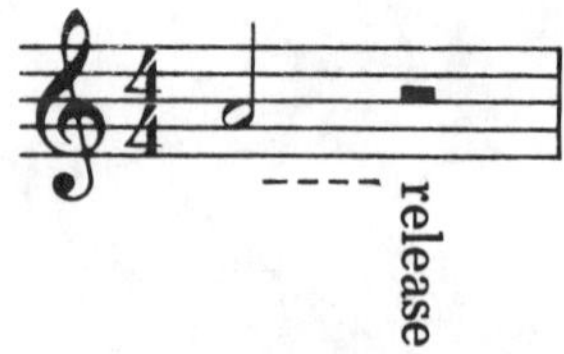

2. At the end of a slur: the key for the last note is released before the key for the next note is depressed, thus slightly shortening its duration.

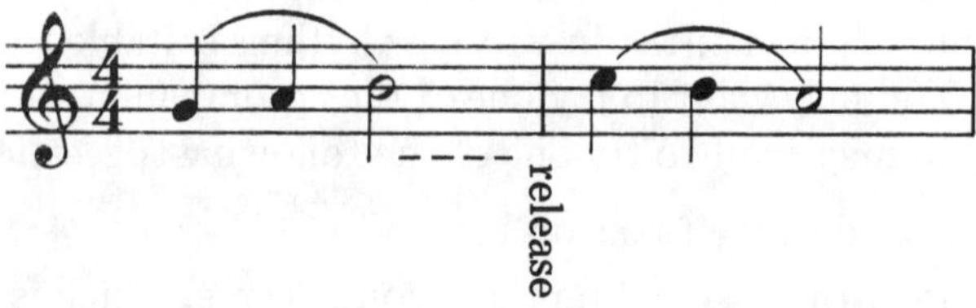

3. When *staccato* or *non legato* appears in the score, or there are staccato dots above or below the notes.

Note: the proportion of sound and silence to be given detached notes may vary with the character of the music. In "March," page 39, the staccato sounds are short and crisp. In measures 1 and 5 of "Minuet," page 39, they are more likely to be longer and gentler in character.

4. When notes are repeated.

On the piano, repeated notes have to be detached. Unless staccato is desired, however, each note should be sustained as long as possible before releasing the key and depressing it again for the next note. In measures 2 and 6 of "Minuet," the *tenuto* sign calls for such sustained touch.

Exercises for Key Release

Tap these three exercises with the second finger of each hand on a flat surface, such as the closed fallboard of the piano or a table. Hands should be resting in playing position.

These photographs show correct and incorrect lifting of the finger for key release.

correct

incorrect

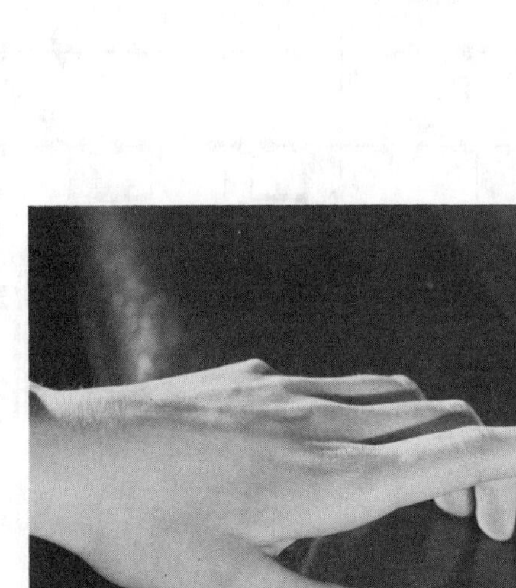

Repeat each measure as many times as necessary for secure timing of finger articulation. Then tap without repeats. (Hold the last whole note for its full value, then release.)

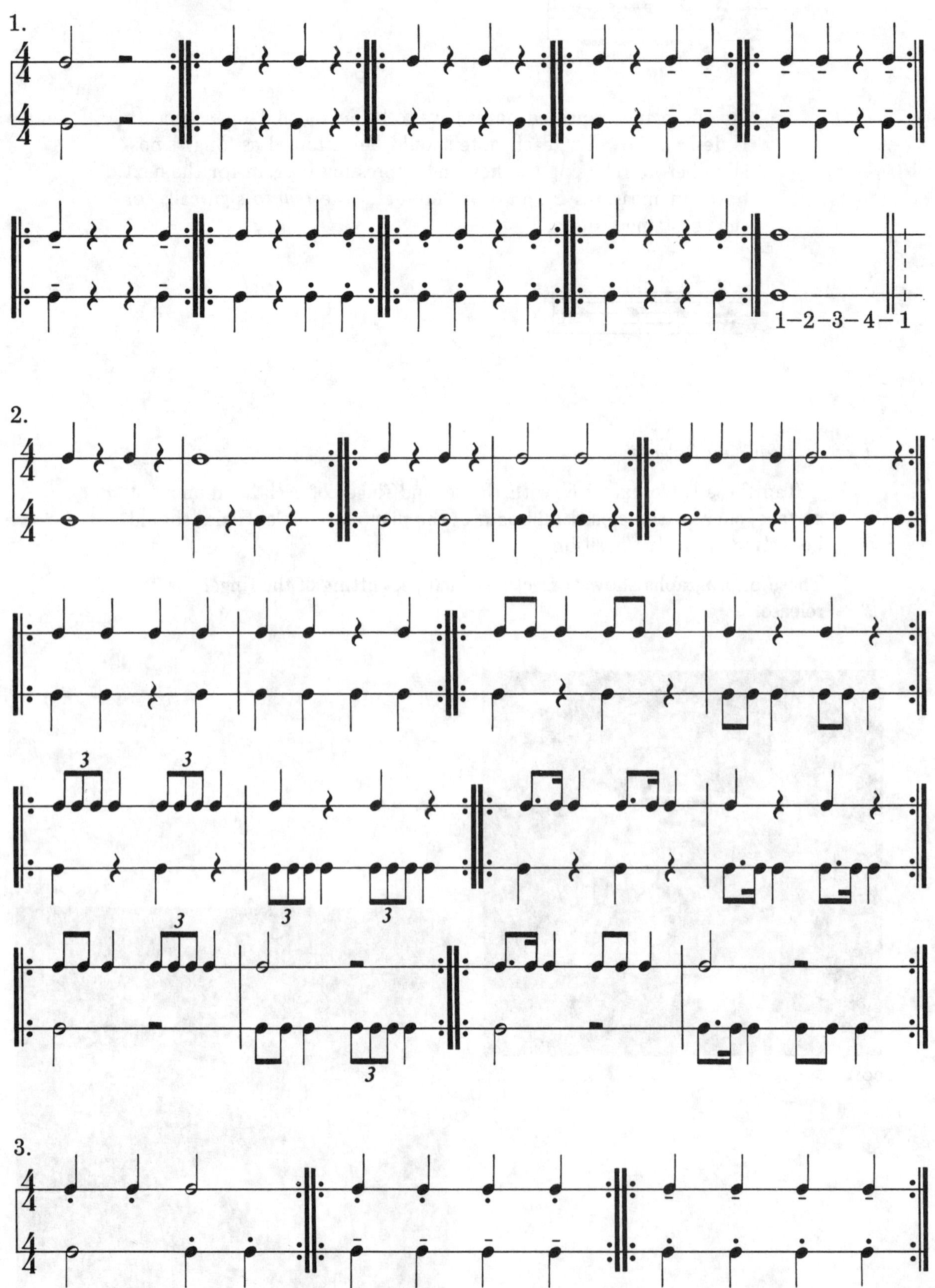

Exercises for Combination of Legato and Staccato

Play these exercises in C, D♭, D, G, A♭, and A major. When you transpose exercise 1, note that the upper voice in the left hand moves up and down by whole steps.

1.

2.

3.

4.

Phrasing and Articulation

Good musical performance makes clear to the listener the shape of each phrase—its beginning, development, and ending.

Usually the development is projected through dynamic shadings of crescendo and diminuendo. The shape also becomes more distinct through articulation. Within a phrase may occur both legato and detached groups of notes.

Phrase beginnings and endings are indicated by judicious use of silence between phrases. This silence may be as long as a rest printed in the score, or as brief as a mere "breathing point."

An Effective Practice Method

To learn to play a composition competently and musically, you should play without mistakes in rhythm, fingering, and notes as nearly as possible from the very first reading of the piece. The following steps will reduce the number of repetitions needed to "get the piece in the fingers."

1. Realize the rhythm as suggested on pages 11-12.
2. Scan the right-hand part to locate hand position(s) on the keyboard (see analysis of positions for the following piece, "Minuet." Place the hand in position, with fingers correctly located on the proper keys. When the hand must find more than one position, practice finding them in succession silently until you can recall them quickly.
3. Play the passage within the first hand position with correct rhythm, articulation, and phrasing, aiming to have it correct the first time.
4. Give yourself time to move to the next position, then play that passage as written. Continue with the remaining positions.
5. Play the entire part for that hand, maintaining a steady beat.
6. Repeat steps 2-5 for the left-hand part. These four steps are the only ones in which attention is directed to each hand alone. From this point on, play hands-together, not separately.
7. Play hands-together slowly enough to maintain the beat. (At this point, you may want to play the part for the right hand while tapping the rhythm of the left hand, and vice versa.)
8. Isolate trouble spots for special attention. Problems might be timing of key release, shifting of hand positions, playing intervals correctly fingered in time, or irregular fingering. You will have eliminated the problem when you are able to play the piece in time from beginning to end.
9. Once you have achieved accuracy at a slow tempo, gradually speed up to the proper tempo. You should be able to do this easily and fairly quickly.
10. At all times, listen! Can the melody be heard? Is it shaped into meaningful phrases? Is the tempo acceptable?

1. MINUET

D. G. Türk
ed. by L. G.

Moderato

Analysis of Hand Positions

Right hand

Left hand

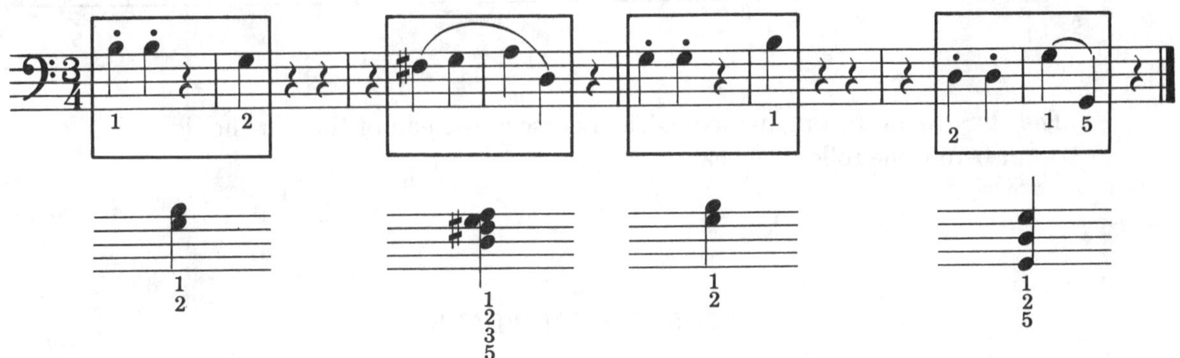

2. MARCH

Türk

Allegro moderato

Türk usually gave no indications for articulation in his pieces, so that performers are free to make their own decisions. Three possibilities for the opening measure of "March" are given below.

3. SYNCOPATION

The slurs are in the original score. The release at the end of the slur should occur before the following beat.

4. THE SHEPHERD PLAYS

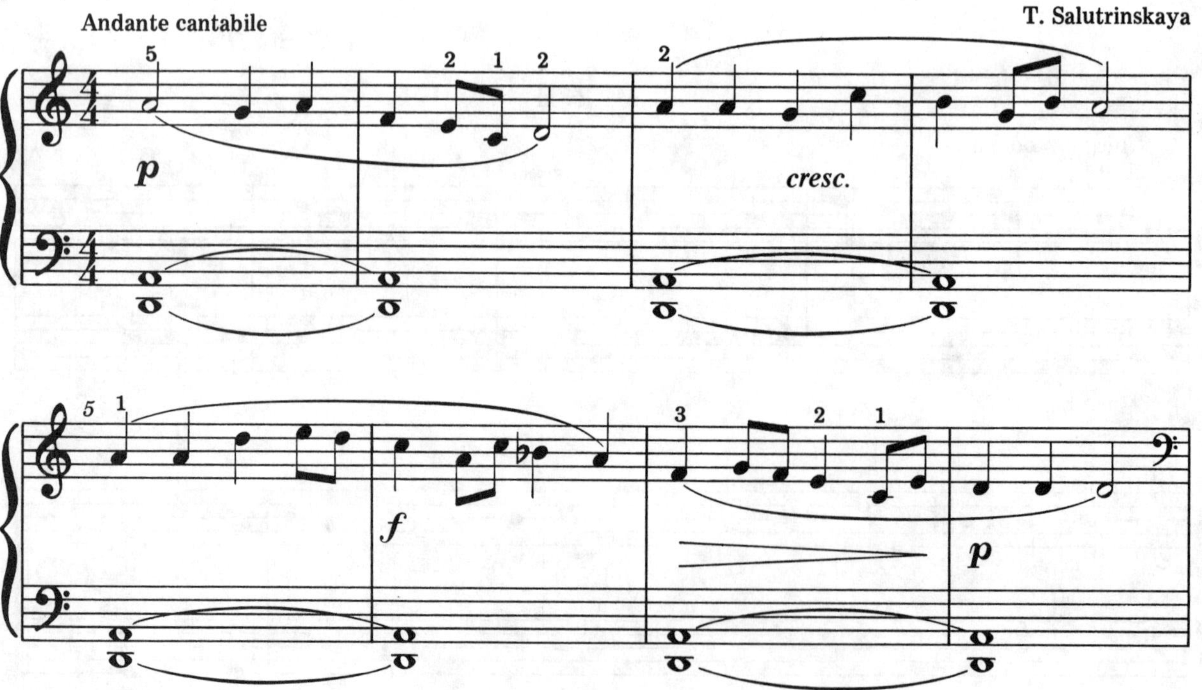

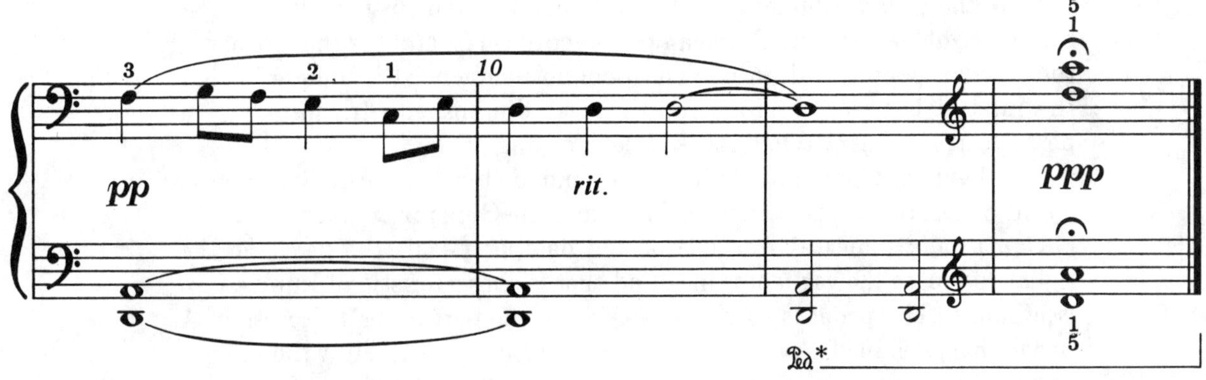

*Depress the damper pedal (the pedal on the right) throughout bars 11 and 12.

5. MASQUE

From *Little Piano Book.* © Copyright 1954 Elkan-Vogel, Inc. Used by permission.

Changing Hand Positions

Selections 6 and 7 require changes in hand position for both hands at the same time. The practice time needed to learn each piece may be reduced by scanning the score to spot these changes, and then by fixing in mind before playing (a) the visual shape of each position on the keyboard, and (b) the tactile sensations of the fingertips touching the proper keys.

In 6, the accompaniment is based on pentachordal clusters. The cluster for the right hand is the Phrygian pentachord on E, and for the left hand, the Locrian pentachord on B. (The Locrian pentachord is unique in that the interval between the root and fifth is a diminished fifth instead of a perfect fifth; it has two half steps instead of one.)

The keyboard position for the left-hand melody is the Lydian pentachord on D; for the right-hand melody, it is the G major pentachord.

Con pedale indicates free use of the damper pedal (the pedal on the right) to create the vagueness in sound that is characteristic of Impressionistic music. The pedal is to be "changed" at the performer's discretion. A pedal change is made by letting the pedal up in order to clear the strings, and then depressing it again.

6. BETWEEN SLEEP AND WAKING

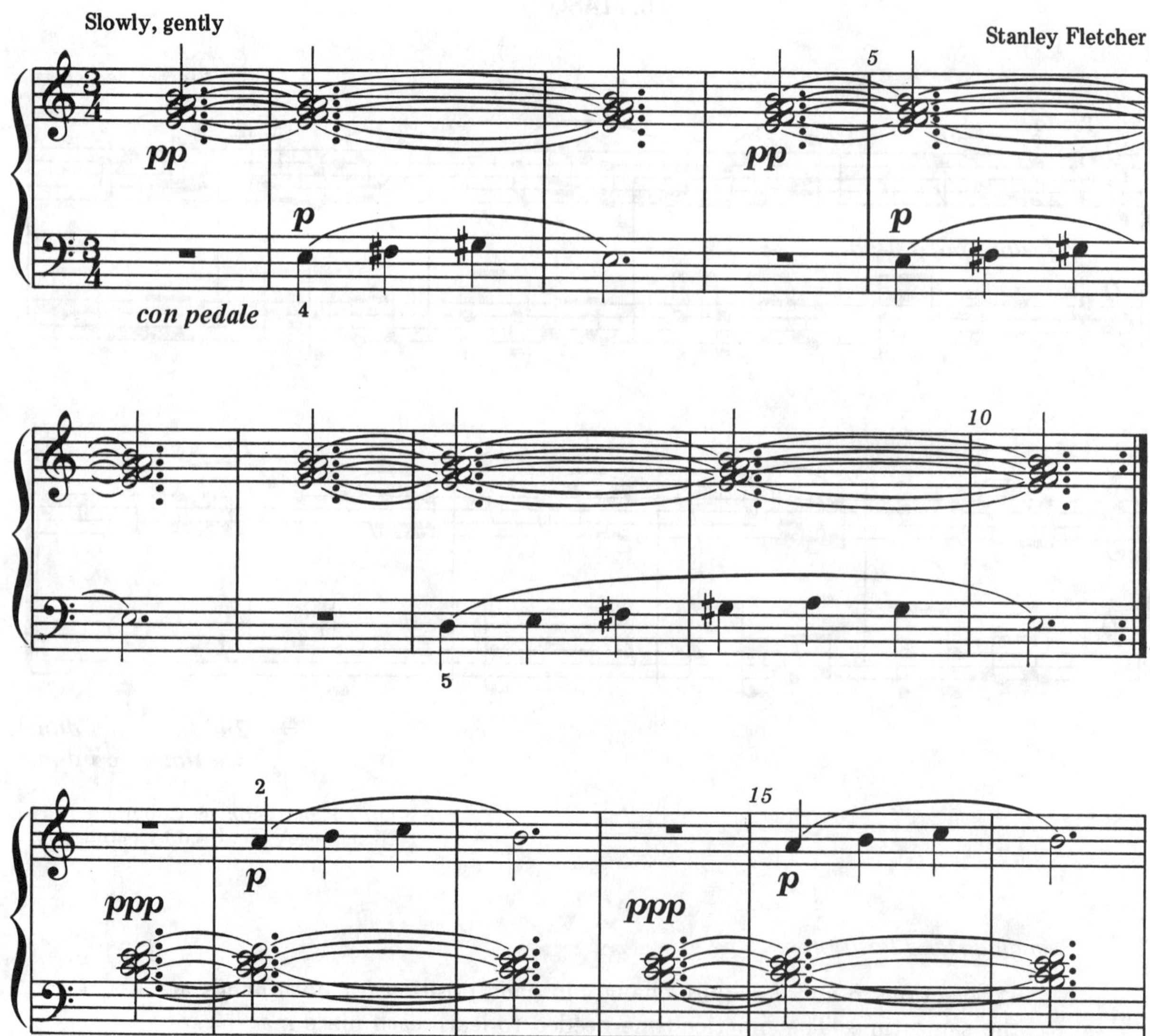

From *Contemporary Collection*, © 1963. Reprinted by permission of Summy-Birchard Company, Evanston, Ill.

20
25
30
ppp
p
4
35
40
ppp

Before playing selection 7, scan and identify pentachords for quick hand placement.

7. SCHERZO ON TENTH AVENUE

From *Contemporary Collection*, © 1963. Reprinted by permission of Summy-Birchard Company, Evanston, Ill.

UNIT FOUR

Playing in Expanded Range

IMPROVISATION

Melody in Changing Hand Positions

Structure Melody based on pentachords with only white keys
Two-measure melodic phrases
Melodic movement predominantly in seconds
Accompaniment: ostinato of perfect fifths

IN DORIAN MODE

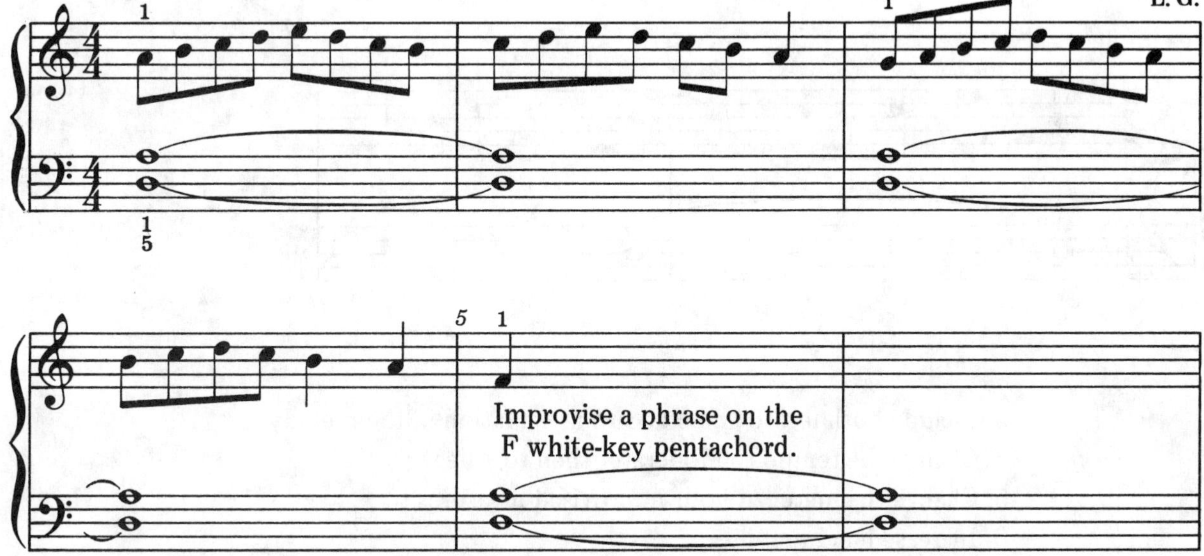

Note: The Dorian mode is based on the eight-tone scale on the white keys from D to D.

Melodic Development

Elaborate on the melodies you just improvised, using the following suggestions if you wish.

1. Create rhythms using a variety of note values.

example

2. Introduce melodic skips within the five-note pattern.

example

3. Include both legato and staccato articulation in the melody.
4. Change the tempo to Moderato, then to Allegro.
5. Change the meter of your improvised measures to $\frac{3}{4}$.
6. Increase hand mobility.

Change the octave register of the left hand in every measure.

Change the register of the melody from one phrase to the next.

7. Develop dynamic color:
   a. Play the first phrase forte, the second piano.
   b. Introduce crescendo and diminuendo within each phrase.

TECHNIQUE

Changing Hand Positions Without Looking at the Keyboard

These two exercises will give you practice in shifting your hands to different positions during rests. You may need to look at the keyboard at first, but the sensations of touch and movement will soon become dependable guides to accuracy.

In 1, note that the right-hand part is notated in the bass clef.

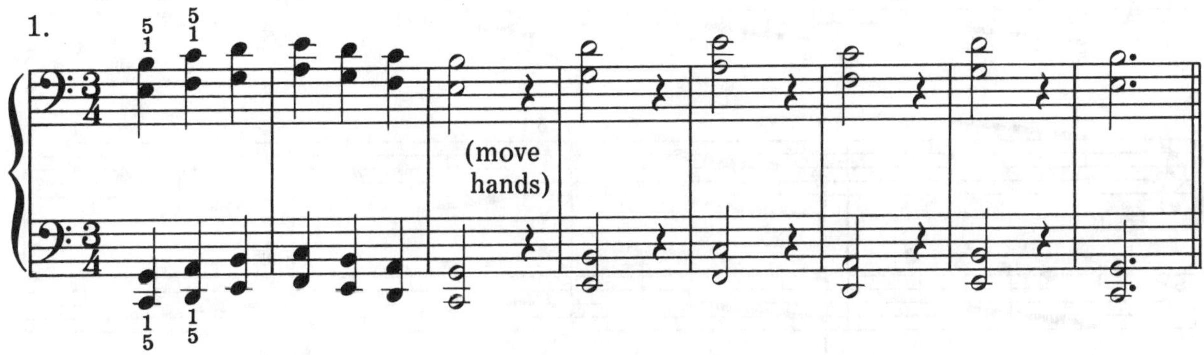

2.

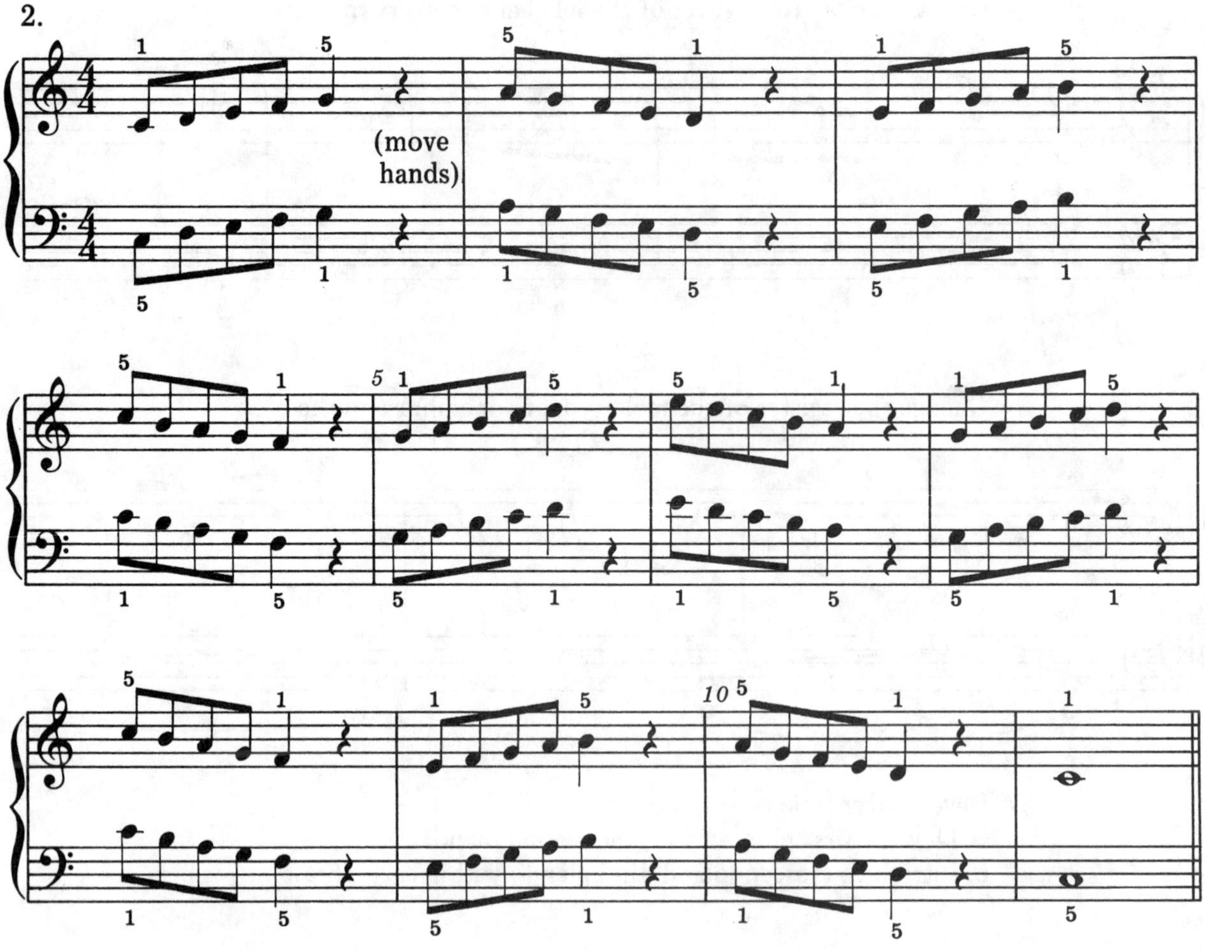

(move hands)

Contracting the Hand from Thumb to Fifth Finger

In the following exercise, shift the right-hand thumb and the left-hand fifth finger on the third beat to be in position for the first beat of the next measure. In measure 7, shift the right-hand fifth finger and the left-hand thumb. Practice without looking at the keys.

Expanding from Thumb to Fifth Finger

Practice without looking at the keys. Shift fingers on the third beat.

Note: It is useful to practice all technical exercises at different dynamic levels, and also to practice crescendo and diminuendo within each pattern. As a first step, practice ascending patterns crescendo (making sure to start the crescendo softly); practice descending patterns diminuendo.

SIGHT READING AND TRANSPOSITION

One Hand in Expanded Range

The following selections have a pitch range wider than the perfect fifth of the tonic pentachord (the five scale degrees from tonic to dominant).

The fingering involves expansion or contraction of the hand to accommodate the extra keys.

For maximum development of reading skill, play hands-together, one octave apart, the first time through. Fingering for the right hand is above the notes; for the left hand, below the notes.

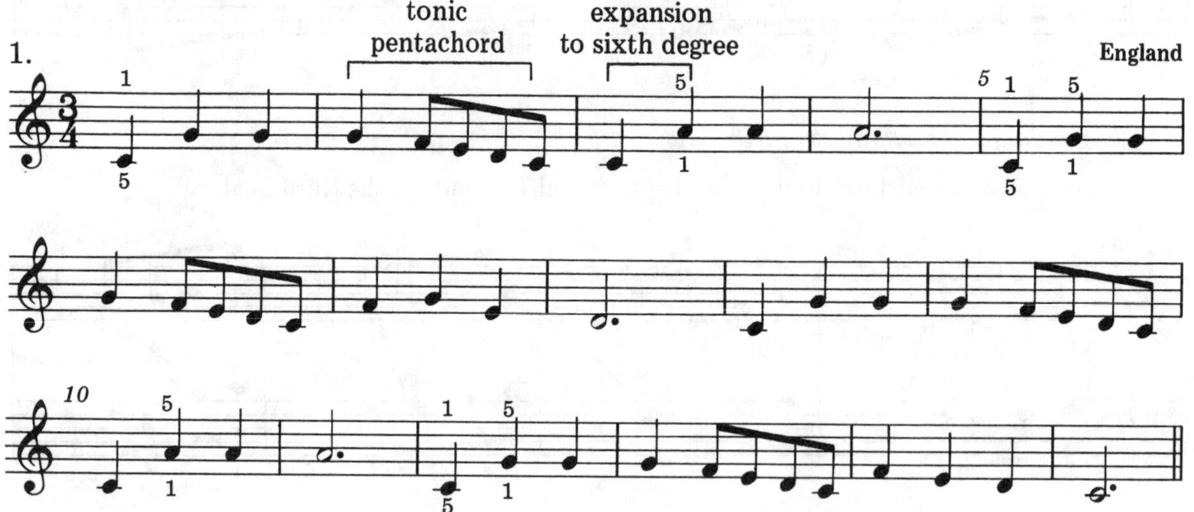

Transpose to G, D, and A. Find the tonic pentachord of the new key, locate the starting pitch of the melody, and read from note to note by interval without looking at the keys. Note that the sixth degree is a whole step higher than the fifth degree.

To develop auditory memory, transpose to D♭ and A♭ by ear. Practice while looking at the keys, then without looking.

Note that 2 is in G. (The note at *Fine* tells you.) Note also that it starts on the third degree of the scale.

Transpose to several other keys. Continue transposition for all selections.

Try to sight read 4 and subsequent selections in some key other than the original.

Exercises 8-11 expand the range to include both the sixth tone and the seventh tone, a half step below the tonic major pentachord.

scale degrees: 7 1 2 3 4 5 6

Three hand positions may thus be involved:

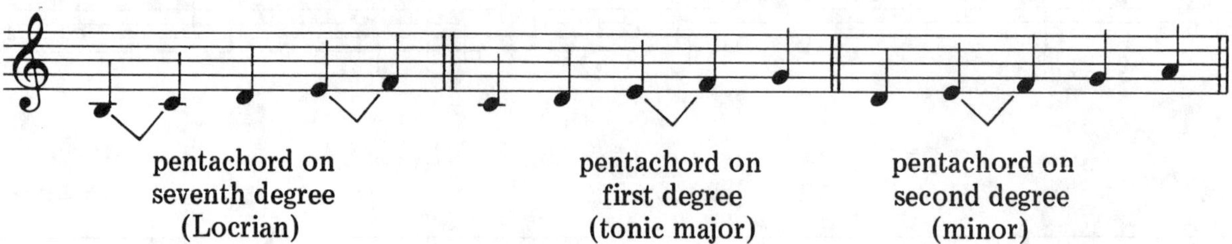

In transposing exercises 8-11, it is helpful to keep in mind that there are four notes of the tonic pentachord that occur in each of the other pentachords. In exercise 8, they occur within the first two phrases.

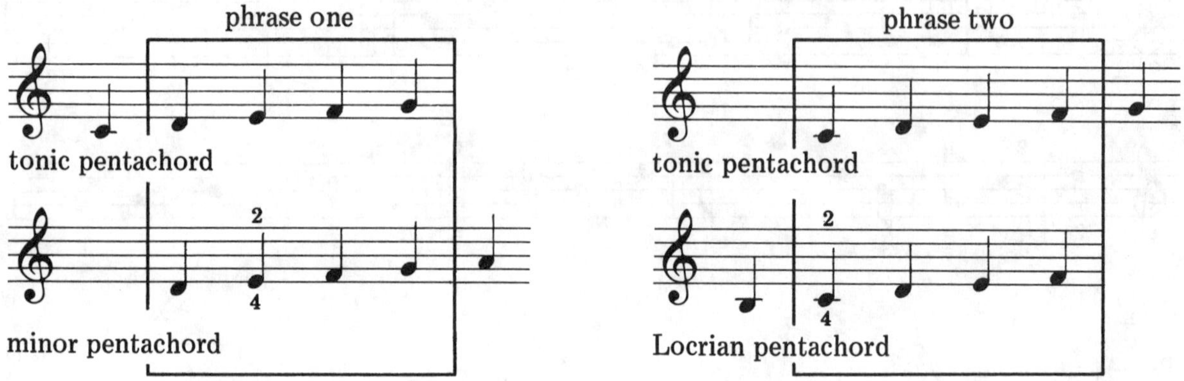

phrase one

tonic pentachord

minor pentachord

phrase two

tonic pentachord

Locrian pentachord

8.

Beethoven

9.

Latvia

Exercise 12 encompasses a pitch range of a sixth, from the dominant (G) to the third degree above the tonic (E). The pentachord on the dominant is major, and the added sixth is a whole step up from the top note in the pentachord. Therefore, in transposing, the first note of the melody, which is the dominant, may be used as the first pitch of a major pentachord, and the transposition continued throughout by interval.

Transpose 12 to hand positions on C, D, D♭, A, and A♭.

Exercise 13 starts on the dominant pentachord and moves to the tonic. Transpose to G, D, D♭, A, and A♭.

13. **British Isles**

Plan fingering for both hands for exercise 14.

14. **U.S.**

Exercises 15-19 are in the minor mode. Note that in these melodies the sixth degree is a half step above the tonic pentachord.

15.

Transpose to d, c, c♯, g, and g♯.*

In 16 and 17, add the proper accidental to the sixth degree. Transpose to a, c, c♯, g, and g♯.

16. **Russia**

*From now on, this book will observe the convention of capital letters for major keys and lower-case letters for minor keys. Thus D and d represent the keys of D major and D minor, respectively.

17. **Latvia**

Exercise 18 includes the seventh tone, but here, a whole step below the tonic. This form of the minor scale is the Aeolian mode. It is also called the *natural minor.*

18. **Latvia**

In exercise 19, the seventh tone is a half step below the tonic pentachord. When that is the case, the scale involved is called the *harmonic minor.*

19. **France**

Rhythm for Two Hands: Tapping

When the eighth note is the unit for counting and the time signature indicates beats in multiples of three per measure (such as $\frac{6}{8}$, $\frac{9}{8}$, $\frac{12}{8}$), the eighth notes are grouped in threes.

The rhythmic accent falls on the first note of each group. Frequently in keyboard music, one hand plays on the accented beat while the other hand plays varied rhythm.

Except in very slow tempos, the character of the rhythm is best maintained by counting the dotted quarter note as the unit.

Preparatory to tapping the following exercises, clap and count this pattern:

First tap the following exercises while counting 1, 2, 3, 4, 5, 6; then tap them while counting 1, 2, with the dotted-quarter note as the unit.

count
1 2 3 4 5 6

count
1 2

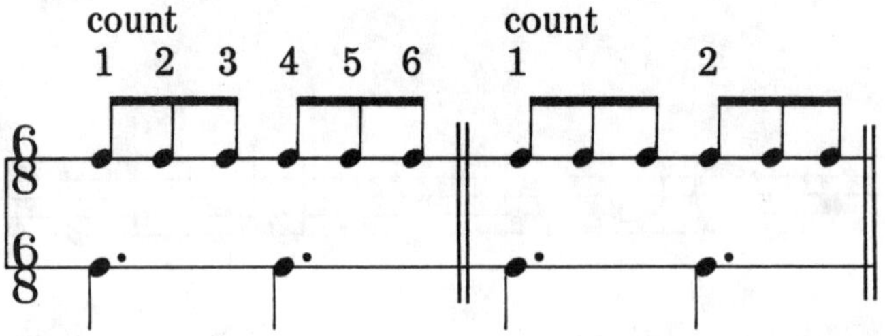

1.

2.

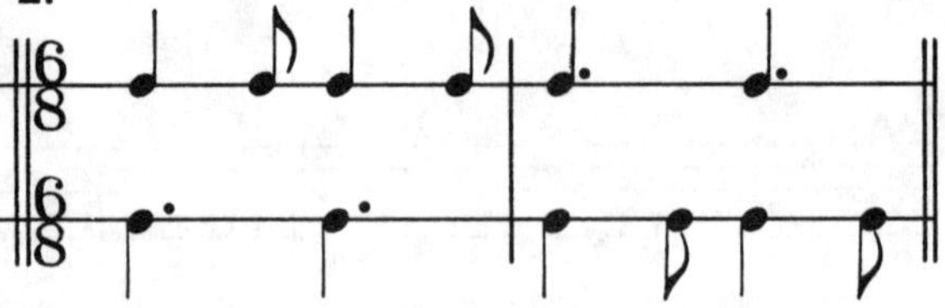

3.

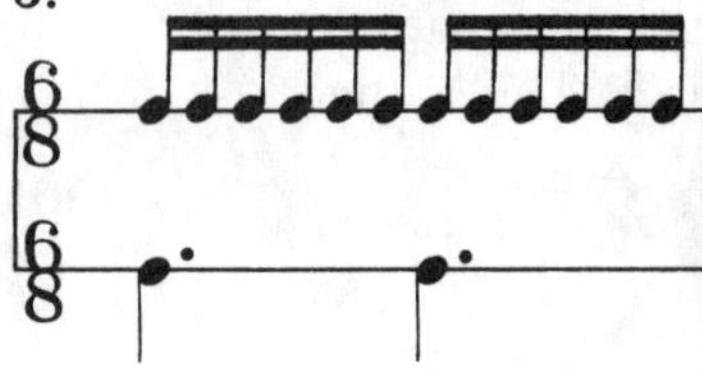

4.

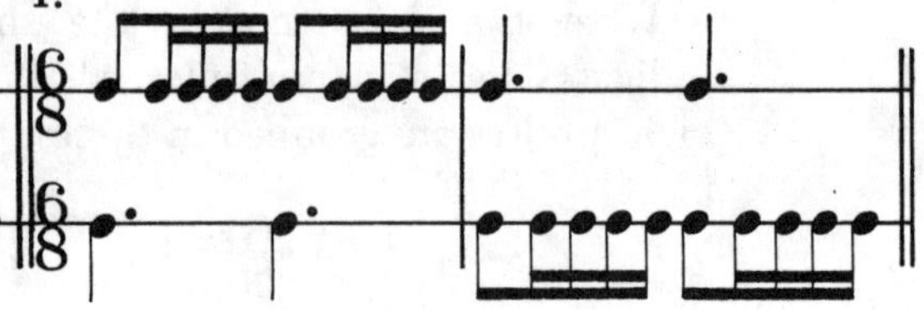

5.

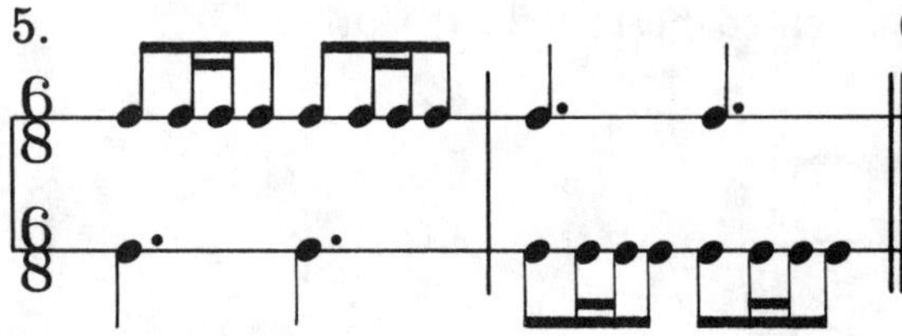

6.

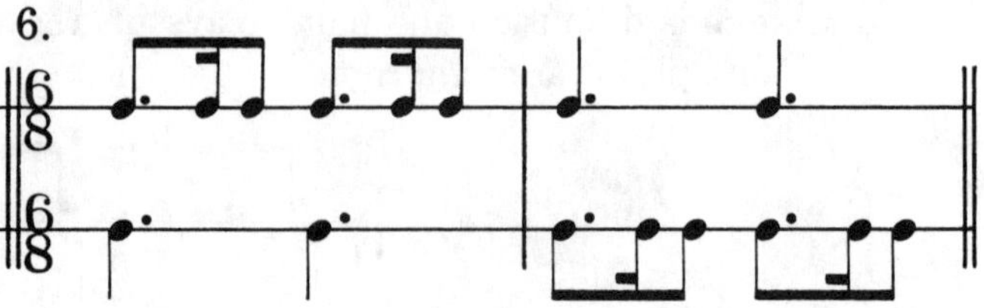

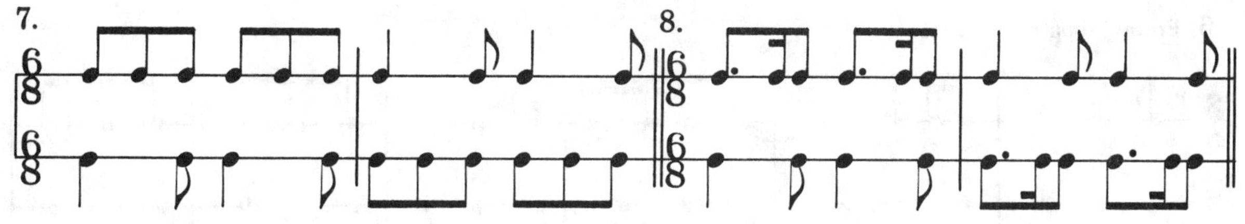

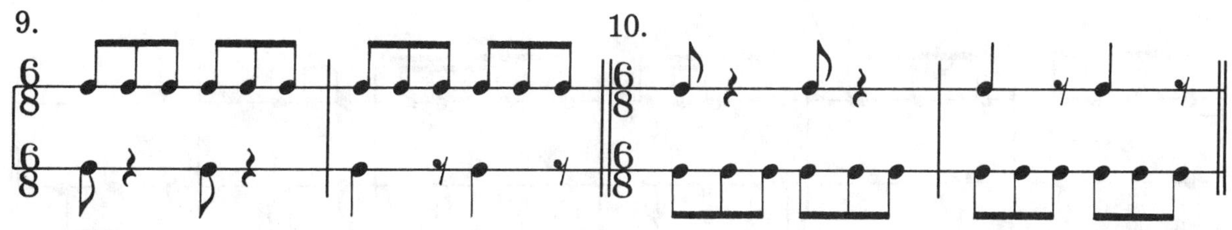

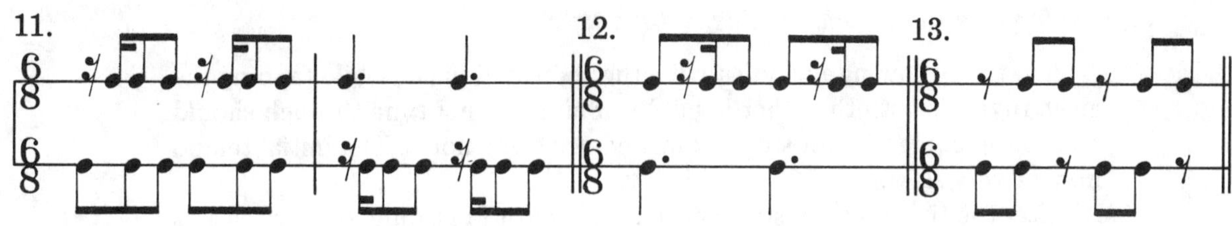

Exercise 14 can be counted with one strong beat per measure.

14. **From "Sonatina," Op. 36, No. 1, Clementi**

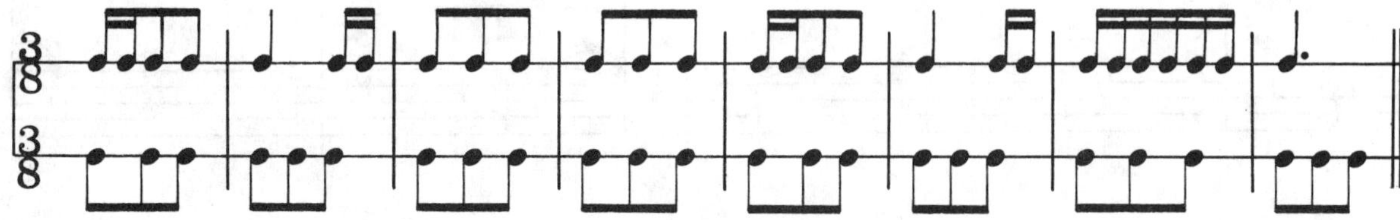

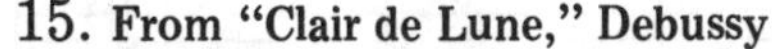

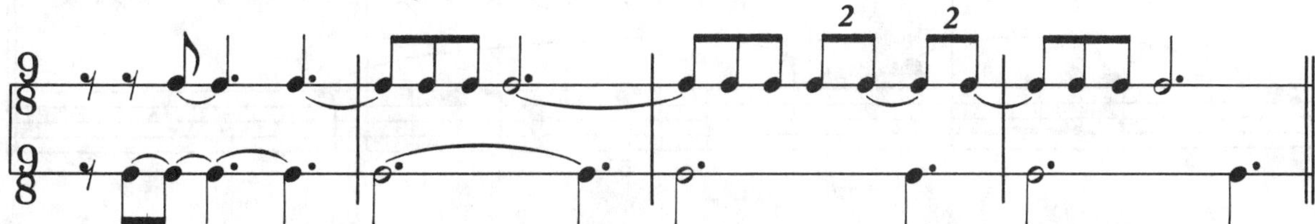

16. From "Sonatine," Ravel

Rhythm for Two Hands: Playing While Tapping

Play the following melodies with the indicated hand, while tapping the given rhythms with the other hand. Your aim the first time through should be to keep going; do not stop for missed or wrong notes. The initial tempo may be very slow.

After the first reading, study each exercise for (1) timing of key releases for staccato, slur endings, and rests; and (2) passages you found technically difficult. Usually the solution is very slow practice to establish correct reflexes.

1.

Giovanni Paisiello

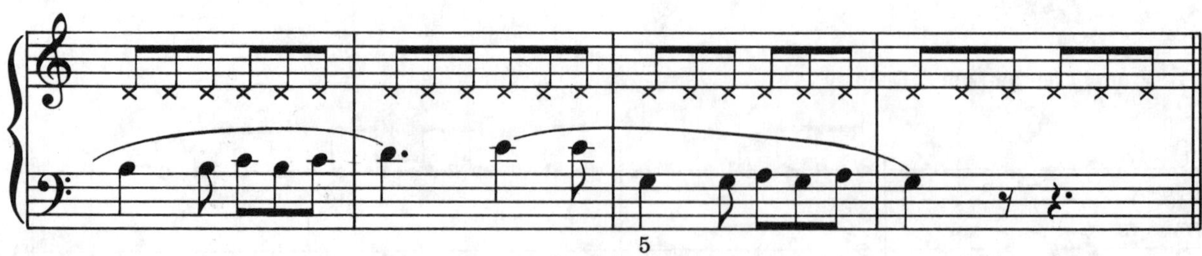

2. Tchaikovsky

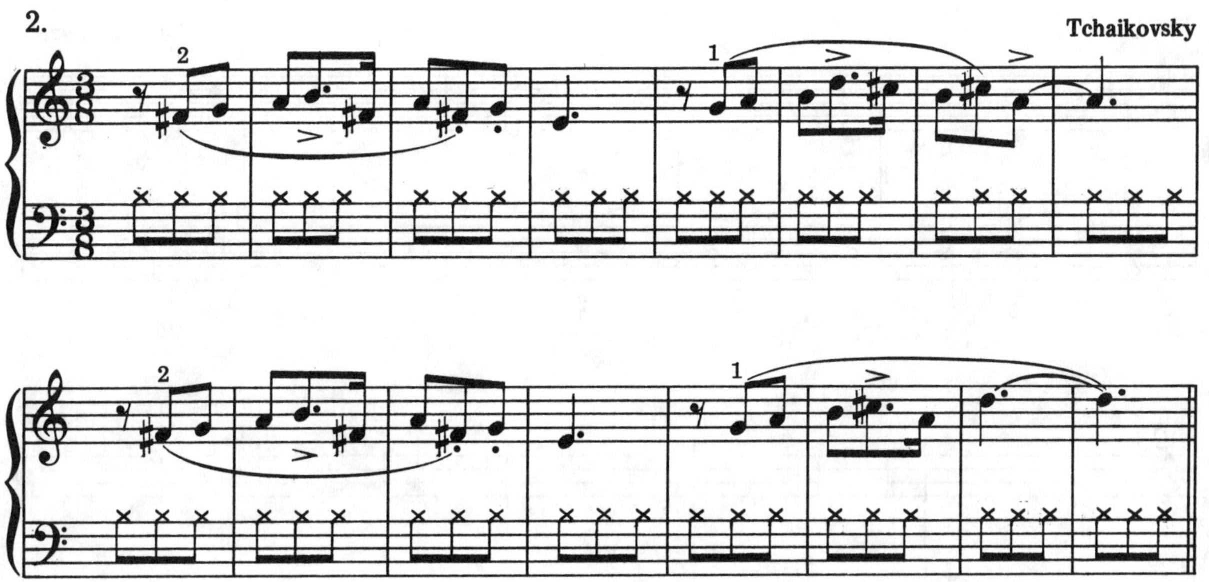

In 3, the hands exchange roles in measure 8. Prepare before playing by finding the keyboard location the right-hand thumb will have to reach on time. Move your hand into position during the second beat of the measure.

Austria
Rhythm from arrangement by Czerny

3.

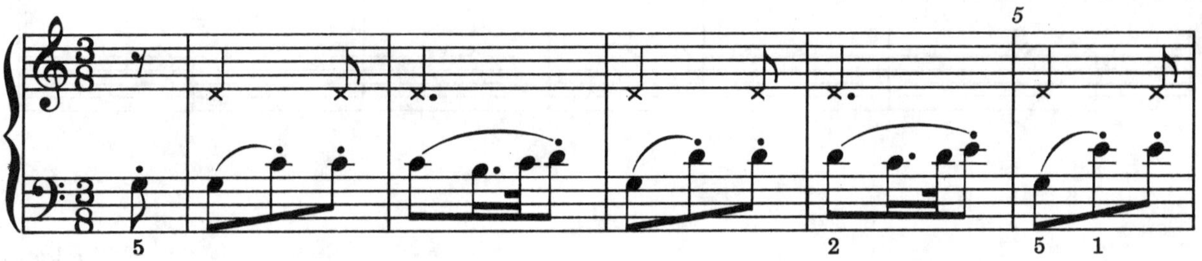

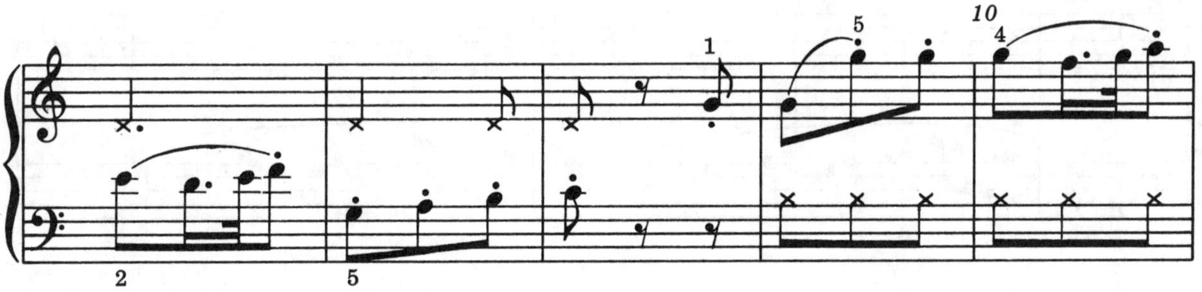

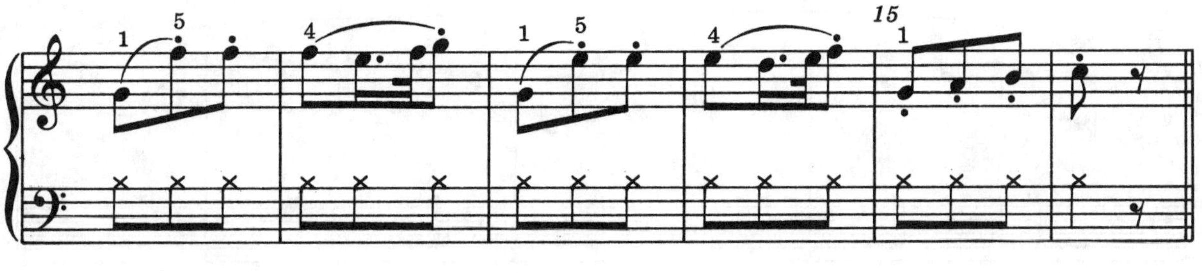

4.
Leopold Mozart
5.
British Isles

6.
Beethoven, Theme from Ninth Symphony
7.
Ireland

8.

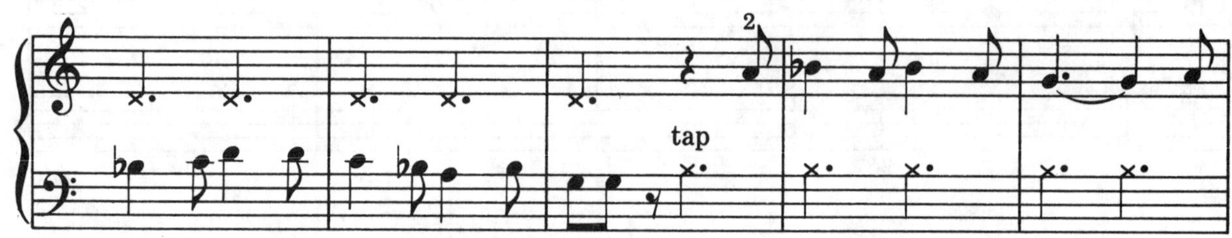

HARMONIZATION AND TRANSPOSITION

Triads on I and V

When you improvised an accompaniment of open fifths for "Joshua Fought the Battle of Jericho" (p. 22), you were harmonizing by an intuitive use of your ear and your imagination. The same is true for the accompaniments you improvised for the melodies in four modes on pages 31-33. Harmonic analysis can help the ear and the imagination in developing the skill of improvising to given melodies.

The basic chord structure used in traditional harmonization is the triad, consisting of root, third, and fifth.

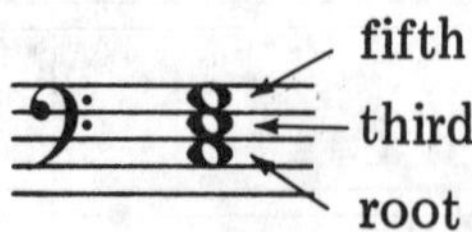

Any scale degree may serve as the root of a triad, and each triad is identified by a roman numeral corresponding to the number of the scale degree.

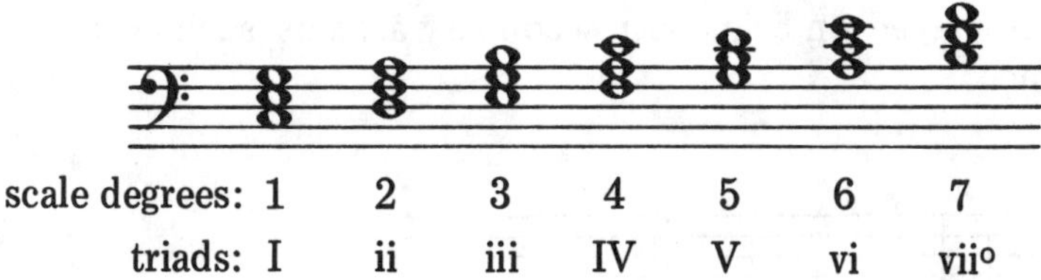

The two most important triads for harmonizing are I and V, the tonic and dominant.

Note that these triads are shown in *root position*—that is, with the root as the lowest note.

In the major mode, both triads I and V are major.

The simplest accompaniment consists of a triad on the strongest beat (the first) of each measure. Select a triad of which one or more of the melody tones are the root, third, or fifth.

MERRILY WE ROLL ALONG

In measure 7, the E on the third beat is a *nonharmonic tone*—that is, it is not a member of the V chord. Nonharmonic tones frequently occur between strong beats, as in measures 1 and 5, in which D is a passing tone between two different chord members.

Triads may also be played on beats with secondary accents, such as the third beat in this tune.

Inversion of V

Since I and V contain a common tone (the fifth degree of the scale), it is convenient for the performer, and results in a pleasing sound, if the chord positions chosen place the common tone in the same voice (continuing line) for both chords. This can be done by using an inversion of the V chord.

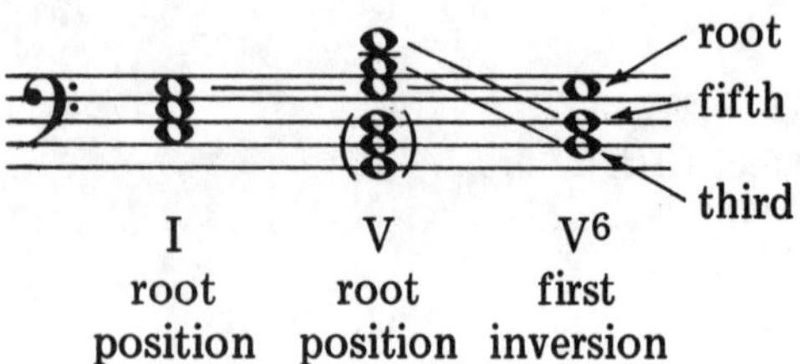

The *first inversion* of V (V^6 or V^6_3) makes the third of the chord the lowest note.

Inversions of V^7

When the melodic line moves from the third scale degree to the second degree (as in measures 2-3 of "Merrily We Roll Along"), parallel octaves occur between the melody and middle voices of the chords.

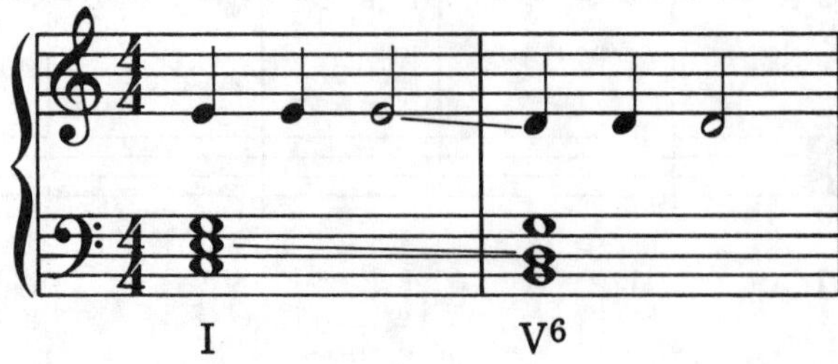

This undesirable sound is avoided if a seventh chord is used instead of a triad on V. A seventh chord on V is created by adding a minor seventh above the root of the triad.

root position

first inversion

Since a seventh chord has four members, one of the members may be omitted in order to maintain the three-voice texture. The root and seventh are essential; hence the omitted member should be either the third or the fifth.

fifth omitted

third omitted

Note that when the third is omitted, the fifth becomes the lowest note of the chord. This is equivalent to the second inversion, or V^{4}_{3}.

For "Merrily We Roll Along," the preferred choice would be to omit the fifth:

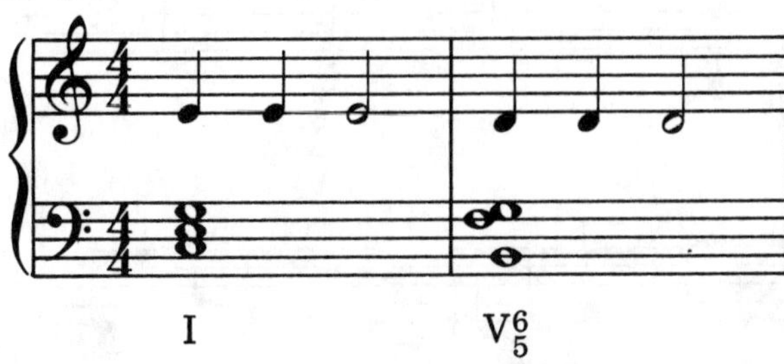

Transposing Melody and Accompaniment

Guidelines for transposing the progression from I to V^{6}_{5}:

> the lower voice goes down a half-step to the seventh degree,
> the middle voice goes up a half-step to the fourth degree,
> the upper voice remains stationary on the fifth degree.

Transpose melody and accompaniment for "Merrily We Roll Along" to all familiar keys: G, D, A, D♭, and A♭.

TECHNIQUE

I-V Progression in Major and Minor

Fingering suggestion: In the right hand, finger all chord tones the same as the fingering for the tonic pentachord, except for the bass voice of V^6 and V^6_5, in which the thumb can move down a half-step.

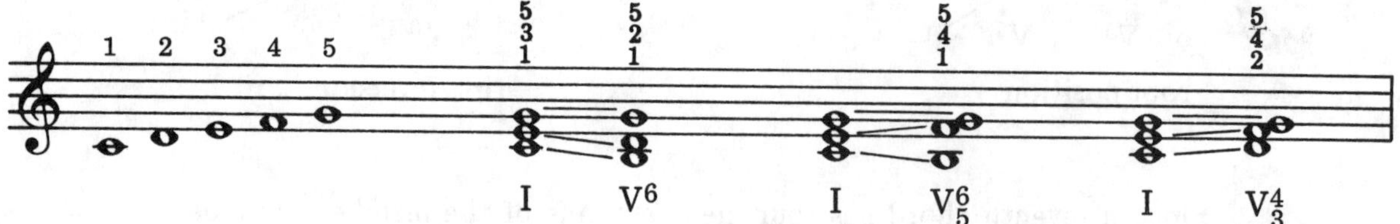

For V^6, in the left hand, the third finger moves to the key occupied by the fourth finger in the major pentachord. For V^6 and V^6_5, the fifth finger moves down a half-step.

Play all exercises in the six major and minor keys previously presented.

1.

2.

3.

HARMONIZATION

Melodies with I and V to Harmonize and Transpose

To determine key, scan for hand position or check the last note. Arabic numbers indicating choice of chord position ($\frac{6}{5}$, $\frac{4}{3}$, etc.) are hereafter omitted; the choice of position and voicing is up to you.

In $\frac{3}{4}$ meter such as in the first exercise, the minimum essential is one chord per measure, played on the downbeat.

In $\frac{6}{8}$ meter, since a chord change frequently takes place within the measure, chords are usually played on the first and fourth beats.

In 3, the melody note on the fourth beat of measure 1 is the fourth degree of the scale, and is also the seventh of the V^7 chord. When the melody moves from the third to the fourth degree, the progression from I to V^6_5 results in parallel octaves. This sound may be avoided by playing V^6 on that beat.

In measure 8, the fifth degree, D, may be harmonized with either I or V. V^6_5 would be a good choice, since it establishes a cadential feeling.

3. **England**

4. **Traditional**

5. **Franz Joseph Haydn**

When the melody is played by the left hand, as in exercise 9, a rhythm pattern of afterbeats in the accompaniment sounds good.

Accompaniment in complementary rhythm is effective for 10. Chords are not played simultaneously with melody notes but on afterbeats, when melody notes are two or more beats in length.

Harmonizing and Transposing in the Minor Mode

As you have seen (p. 55), in the natural minor scale, the seventh degree is a whole tone lower than the tonic.

In many folk melodies in the Western musical tradition, the seventh degree is raised a half-tone.

The scale in which the seventh tone is raised is the harmonic minor.

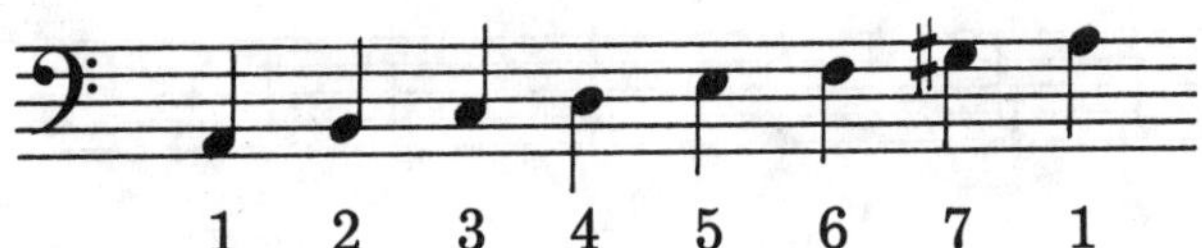

The common practice in harmonizing melodies in minor is to raise the seventh tone in chords. The dominant triad thus becomes major (shown by an upper-case Roman numeral), while the tonic triad is minor, indicated by a lower-case numeral.

The dominant seventh chord thus becomes identical in major and minor.

Exercise 1 offers a number of options for harmonization, such as choice of V or V^6_5 to vary the sound in measures 2 and 3, and choice of harmonizing all C's in the melody or treating some of them as nonharmonic tones.

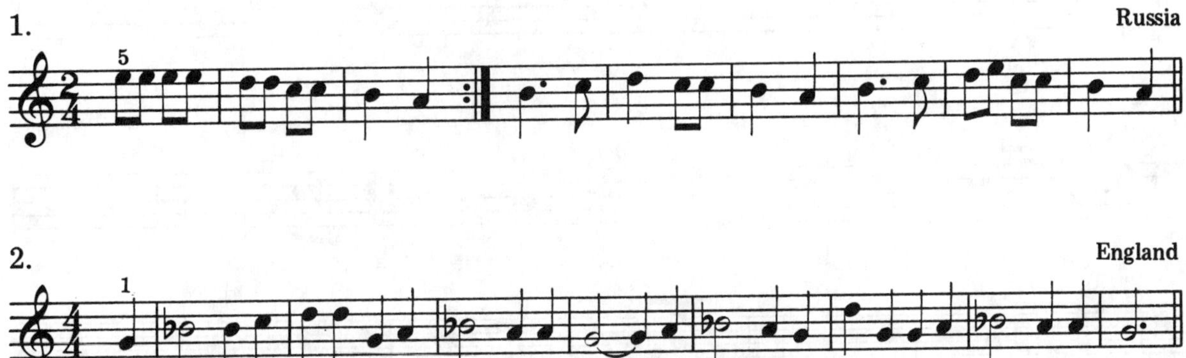

Exercise 3 offers choice of i or V in measure 2. For a final cadence, i^6_4 (second inversion) followed by V^7, resolved to a third, is a commonly used, effective voicing.

i
i6 4
V7
i

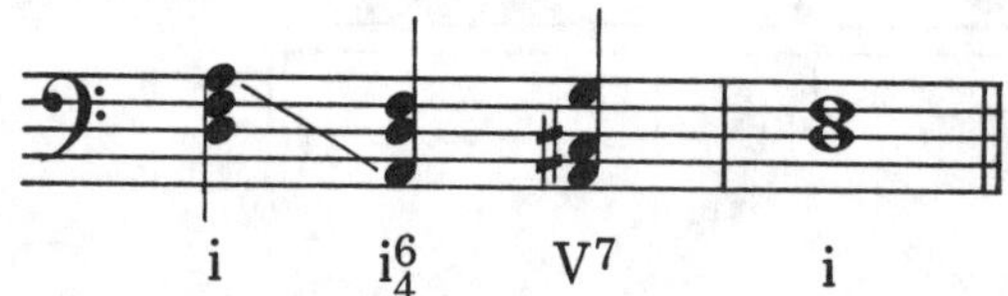

3. **Hebrew**

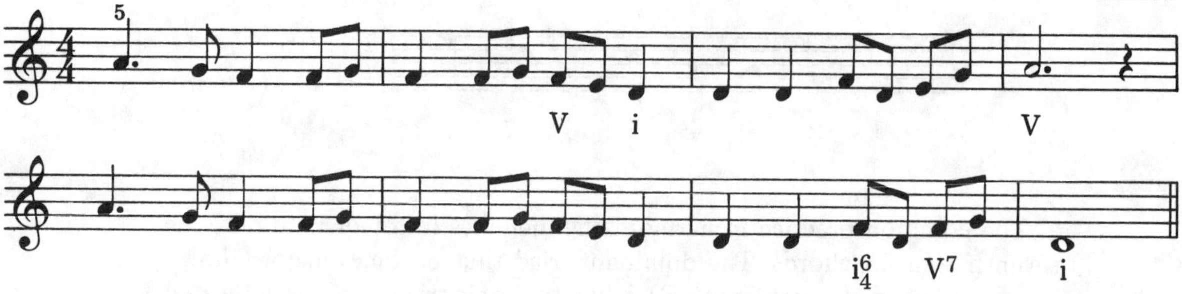
5
V
i
V
i6 4
V7
i

4. **Russia**

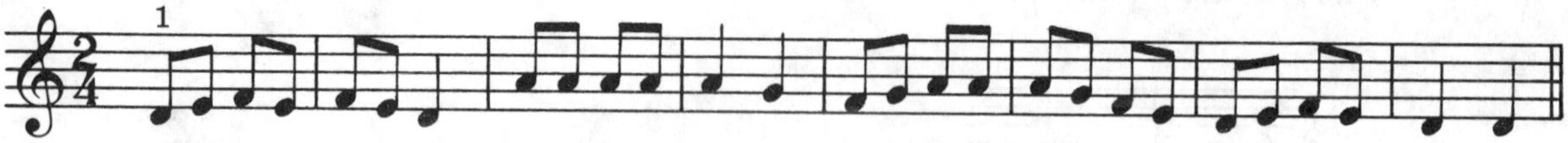
1

5. **Sweden**

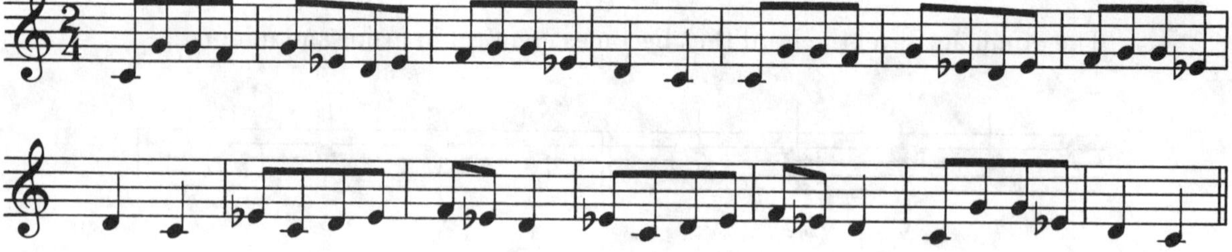

6. **Russia**

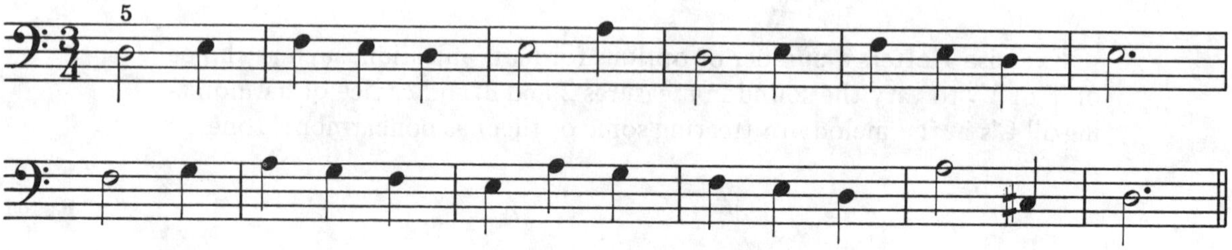
5

7. **France**

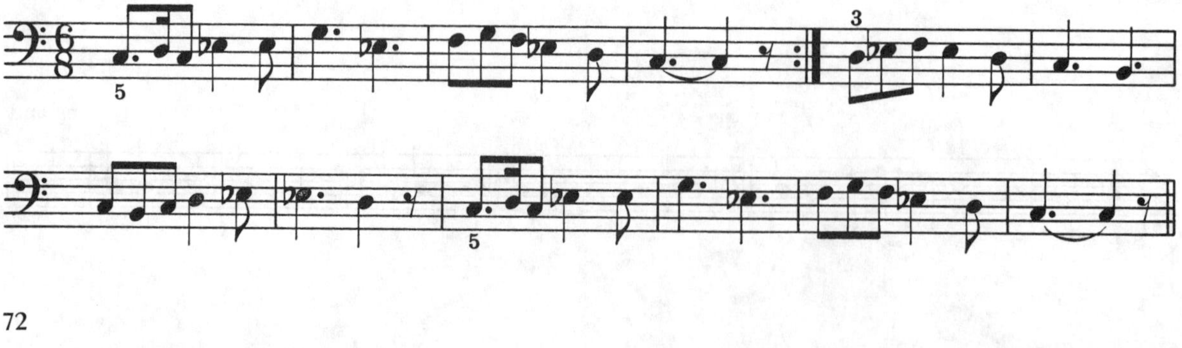
5
3
5

8. France

Exercise 9 is based on the melodic minor scale, in which the sixth *and* seventh degrees are raised a half step in the ascending form.

D natural minor scale D melodic minor scale

In this German dance, Beethoven used only i and V^7 in the accompaniment. Harmonize and transpose to other minor keys.

9. Beethoven

REPERTOIRE

Compositions in Wide Range

When wide leaps occur, prepare for them silently before playing. Suggested steps:

1. Name each note by letter. It takes a long time to learn new notes; they can become more familiar and more quickly identified in each new piece.

Note on extreme high and low ranges: Notes on ledger lines and spaces are best approached intervallically, by using a familiar note as a focus.

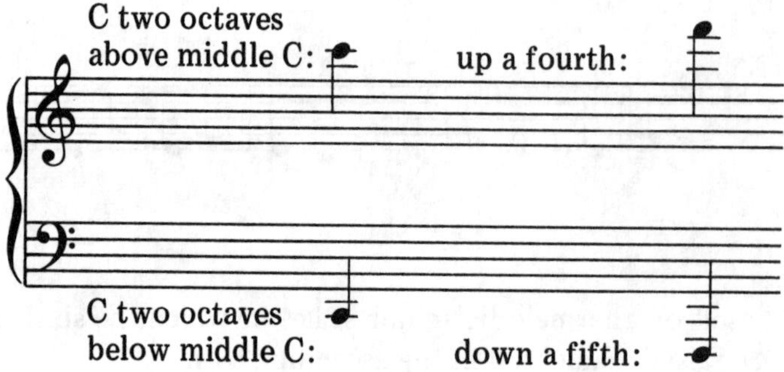

Frequently the symbol *8va* is used. When placed above a note, that note is to be played an octave higher than written; when placed below the note, it is to be played an octave lower. *8va* - - - - - - - - indicates that all notes are played up or down an octave for the duration of the dotted line. *Loco* indicates a return to the normal range following a passage of *8va* notes (see the following piece, "Movement in Whole Tones").

2. Go through the selection, looking at the piano key for each note. Fix the keyboard location firmly in your mind.
3. Go through it again, touching each key with the proper finger.
4. Simulate playing on the closed fallboard or frame of the piano, counting aloud as you move your hands in time in the direction of the keys to be played.

MOVEMENT IN WHOLE TONES

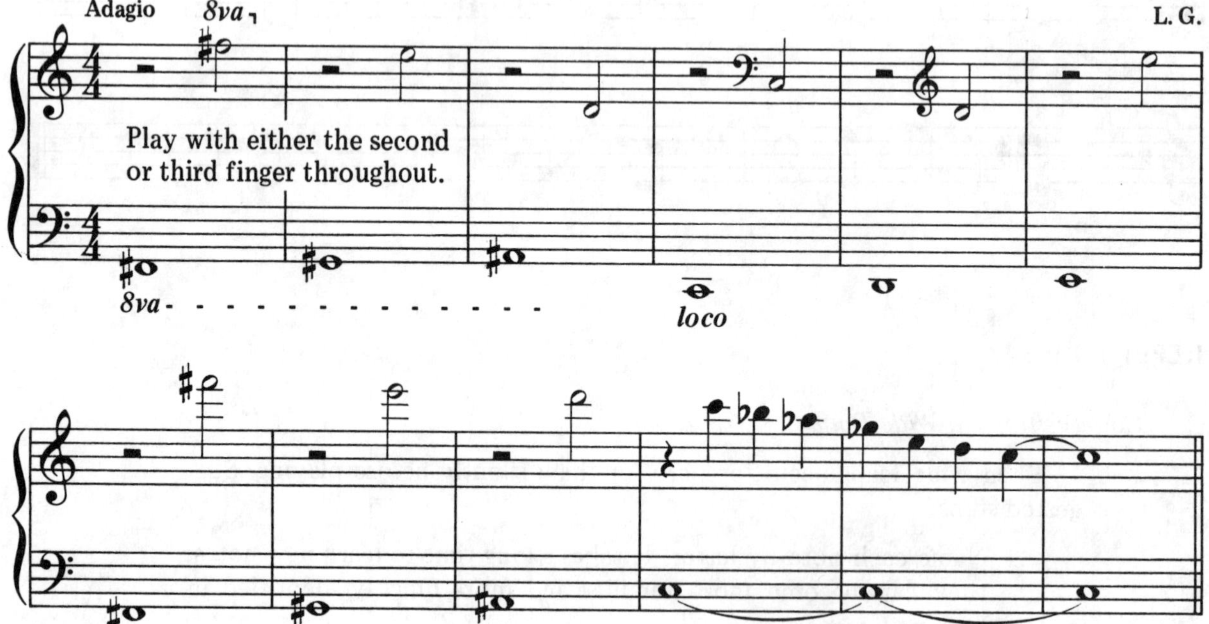

In the next selection, *Pedal* └───┘ indicates usage of the damper pedal. Depress it at the beginning of the beginning of the marking (└───) and hold it down the full duration of the marking. In measure 4, it should be released exactly as the first key is depressed (see p. 41).

COLOR PIECE

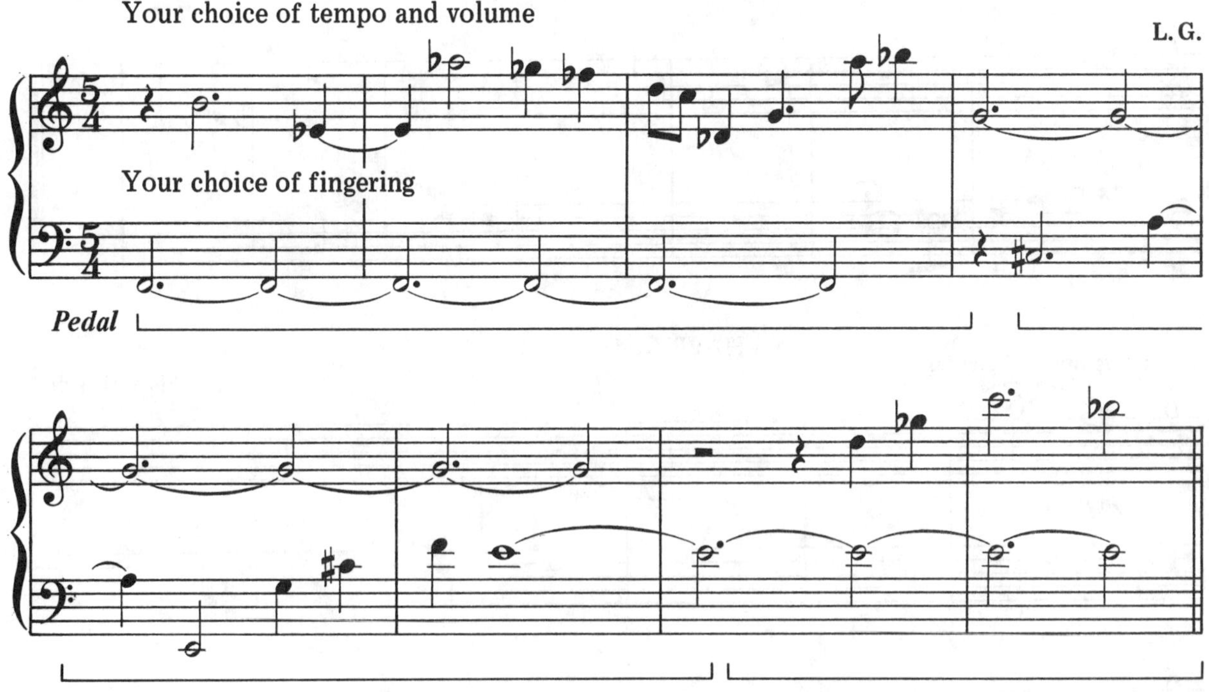

BLACK BECOMES WHITE

IN LOCRIAN MODE
Andantino
L. G.
HAPPY-GO-LUCKY
Easygoing and playful
Sr. Mary D. Wood
mf
R.H.
L.H.
8va
15
(down two octaves)

FOR THE KID NEXT DOOR
(Für's Nachbarkind)

Soulima Stravinsky

From *Piano Music for Children*, Vol. I, by Soulima Stravinsky. Copyright © 1960 by C. F. Peters Corporation, 373 Park Avenue South, New York, New York 10016. Reprint permission granted by the publisher.

SIGHT READING

Ledger Lines

Scan for finger placement. Hear rhythm and pitch movement mentally before playing.

8.

Hand-to-Hand Reading

In the following exercises, both hands play in pentachord positions. Many of the positions have not occurred before in this book.

Before playing, scan the part for each hand for the lowest and highest notes and for accidentals. Play each pentachord and identify its mode by ear. If you cannot decide on the mode, analysis may be utilized.

Summary of Modal Pentachord Structures

Lydian	half step between scale degrees 4 and 5
Major	half step between 3 and 4
Minor	half step between 2 and 3
Phrygian	half step between 1 and 2
Locrian	half step between 1 and 2, and between 4 and 5

Note: Dorian (see pp. 45-46) has the same initial pentachord as minor.

In reading, aim to keep time without hesitation, with intervals as nearly accurate as possible the first time through. Be sure to check the clef.

Write the name of the pentachord in each blank.

1.

Continue as in exercise 1.

2.

4.
5
5
5.
6.
5
5

7.

8.

Germany

9.

Russia

10.

11.

12.

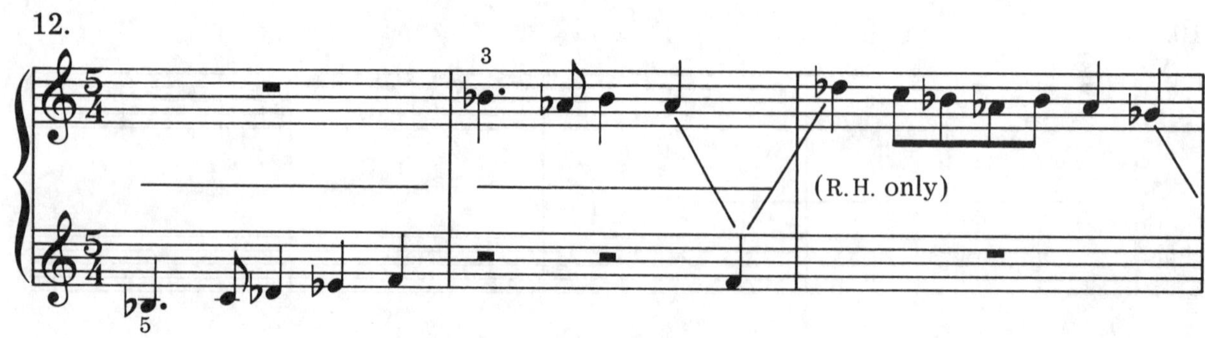

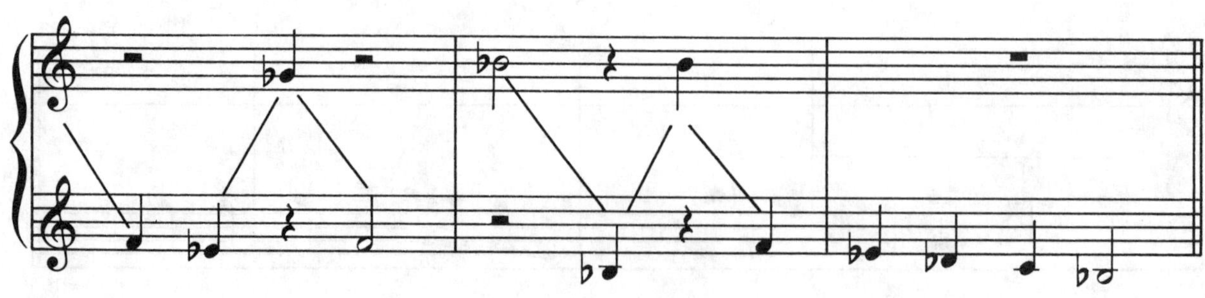

Hands Together in Unison

Selections 13-16 are Primo and Secondo parts of duets. One part is in parallel motion in pentachord positions, with occasional changes within the position. That part is to be sight-read by the class as an ensemble, with the other part to be played by the instructor or one class member. Scan before playing for location of repeats and rests.

13. MELODIOUS PIECES, Op. 149, NO. 8

1.
2.
25
30
35
I
II
p
dolce
f
dim.
sf

14. ALLA MARCIA

Ruthardt

10
I
II
p
poco
a
poco
cresc.
15
pesante
ff
sf

15. SCHERZO, OP. 149, NO. 6

8va
I
II
p
f
Fine
20
25
30

TRIO
8va
35
p
f
I
TRIO
II
40
45
cresc.
Da Capo al Fine

16. SCHERZO, OP. 149, NO. 16

Diabelli

8va
5
20
I
p
1
II
pp
8va
25
mf
8va
30
f
f

8va
35
I
II
p
8va
40
mf
8va
45
1.
2.
f
Fine
1.
2.
f
Fine

TRIO
8va
50
I
p
TRIO
II
p
8va
55
mf
8va
60
f
f

8va
65
I
II
p
70
75
cresc.
f
1.
2.
Da Capo al Fine

Hands Together in Contrary Motion

Exercises 17-20 are in contrary motion, with identical intervals and rhythm in both hands. Hence, the same fingers are playing at the same time in both hands, except at the final cadence.

No key signatures are given. Both may be played in either major or minor mode.

17. **Switzerland**

18. **Austria**

Exercises 19 and 20 should be played in the two pentachords possible for each mode in the given notation. For example, 19 may be played in E and E♭ major, and in E and E♭ minor. Find this new position by the correct sequence of whole and half steps. (See p. 79 for the structure of the major and minor pentachords.)

Hands Together in Homophonic Texture

Selections 21-24 are in homophonic texture (see p. 11), with melody in pentachordal range and accompaniment in a constant position. To make reading easier, tap the parts for both hands simultaneously before playing.

21. MEMORIAL CEREMONY DANCE (YUMAN TRIBE)

Arthur Hollander

From *Indian Drum Beats.* Copyright © 1956 by Belwin, Inc. Used with permission. All rights reserved.

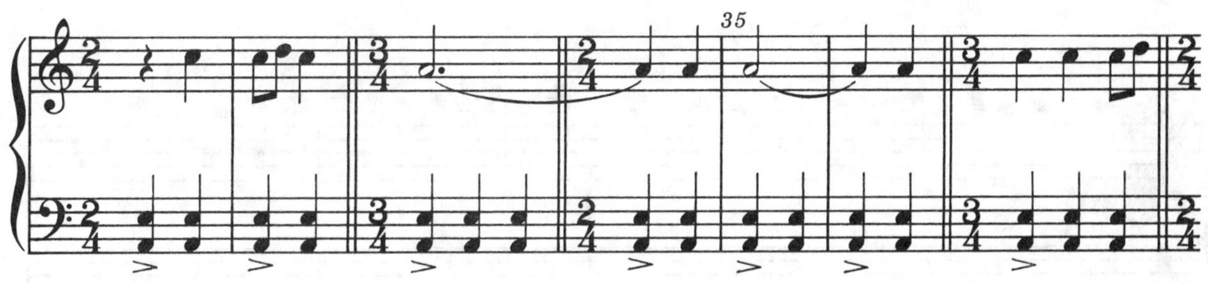

Transpose to other minor keys.

Selection 22 should be played in A and A♭ major.

Transpose to other major keys.

Selections 23 and 24 require more visual attention to the accompaniment, which means that looking ahead is essential.

Practice scanning ahead at least two measures of the accompaniment while playing, keeping them in mind while you focus on the melody. Develop the habit of keeping your eyes ahead of your hands. The eyes should not be fixed on a note until it is played but should be looking one to four notes ahead as you mentally identify the intervals to be played in succession. The larger the number of notes you can retain mentally, while keeping track of tempo, the more freedom you have to direct two hands at once.

23.

Russia
arr. by L. G.

Andante

repeat Allegretto

24.

Transpose 24 to other keys. Notice that the highest note in the right hand is two octaves above the lowest note in the left hand. Find correct positions by maintaining the required succession of major and minor seconds and thirds. Note the augmented second in the position for the left hand, measure 2.

Hands Together in Contrapuntal Texture

Selections 25-30 are in contrapuntal texture, requiring swift identification and accurate performance of two intervals at once—one in each hand.

In selection 25, which is in parallel motion in sixths, the intervals and rhythm are identical for both hands, except at the final cadence. The challenge is to change hand positions on time.

25. LITTLE SCHERZO

Selections 26-30 should be sight-read hands-together, maintaining the beat and never stopping to correct errors. Set the tempo as slow as is necessary to accomplish this.

If you cannot play both hands at sight, do not try to play each hand alone. Rather, resort to reading hands-together in primary movement. A *primary movement* is one which is made for the first time. In reading hands-together, two such movements must be made simultaneously. When these movements are repeated, they become conditioned reflexes, and with practice they become more secure.

When you read in primary movement, aim to play every note correctly with the correct finger, not allowing yourself to play even one note incorrectly. Take enough time to insure accuracy, without maintaining the beat at first. Going through a selection or passage this way once may be enough; after two or three times at most, try playing at a slow tempo, maintaining the beat.

Selections from *The First Term at the Piano*

Béla Bartók

26.

27.

28.

Moderato

5

f

5

29.

Moderato
f

30.
Andante
Latvian melody
arr. by L. G.
p
mf

Transpose selections 25-30 to other keys to reinforce interval reading and to become more familiar with the keyboard patterns of tonality and modes in all keys.

UNIT FIVE

Using Key Signatures

The System of Key Signatures

There are fourteen traditional signatures in use in Western music, containing from one to seven sharps and from one to seven flats.

In writing the conventional signatures, the identity and order of the sharps or flats in each signature is always the same. For example, if there are five sharps, they will always be F, C, G, D, and A, placed in that order on the staff. And if there are five sharps, the same black and white keys will be always associated with that signature.

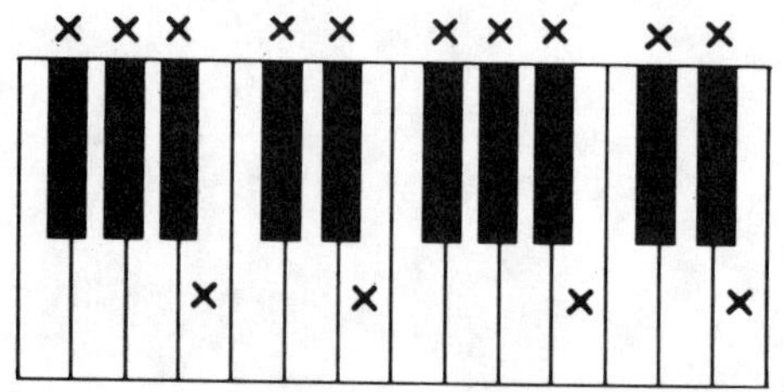

Keyboard pattern for the key signature
with five sharps

In mastering key signatures at the piano, the most useful first step is to associate each key signature with the major and minor scales to which it belongs. (A key signature can also be associated with five other modes; see p. 159.) As you play the following exercises, refer to the table of key signatures on page 111.

Exercise for Major Signatures

As you play each note, recite aloud the name of its major scale and key signature: "C Major, no sharps or flats; G Major, one sharp," and so on, continuing up the keyboard to C♯, seven sharps. Return to low C♭, whose key signature has seven flats, progressing up the keyboard to C, no flats.

Play notes with stems down with the left hand; stems up with the right hand.

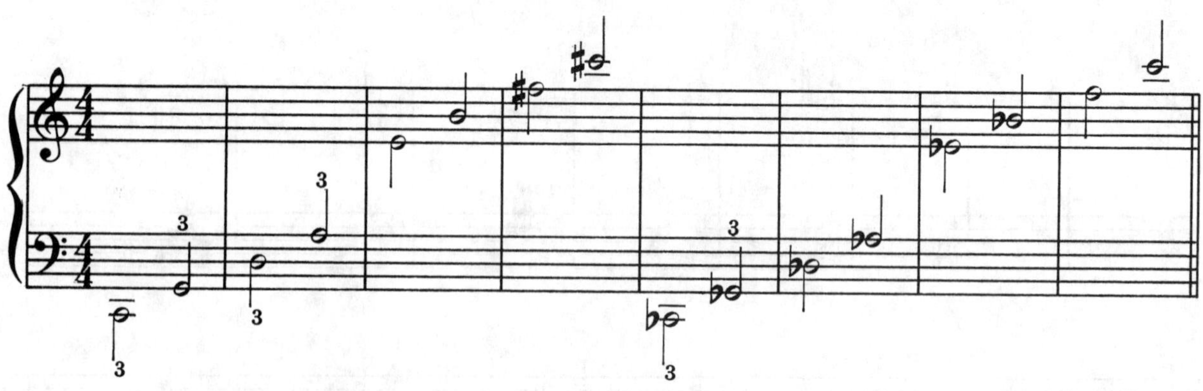

Three of the scales exist in *enharmonic pairs:* that is, the pitches and keyboard tracks are identical for both members of each pair, but the notation is different.

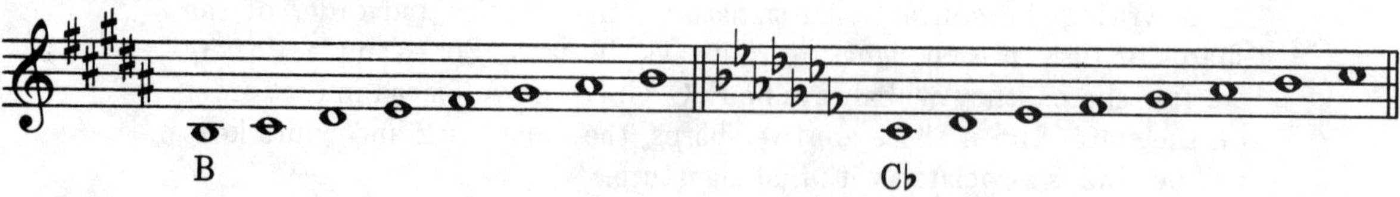

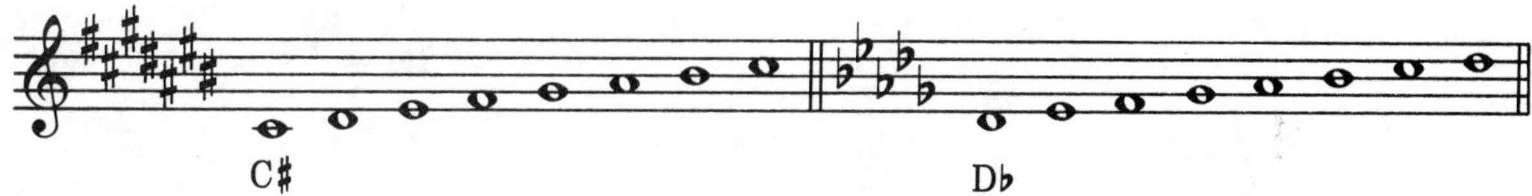

Exercise for Relative Major and Minor Signatures

The relative minor of a major scale begins on the sixth degree of the major scale, or three half steps below the major tonic. Recite aloud while playing: "C Major—A Minor, no sharps or flats," and so on. (Stems down, play with left hand; stems up, right hand.)

The Cycle of Fifths

Note that as one sharp is added, or one flat taken away, the scales occur in a sequence of perfect fifths, generally referred to as the Cycle of Fifths. Knowing the alphabets of perfect fifths is useful in identifying key signatures, position of triads, and the progression from tonic to dominant in all major and minor keys.

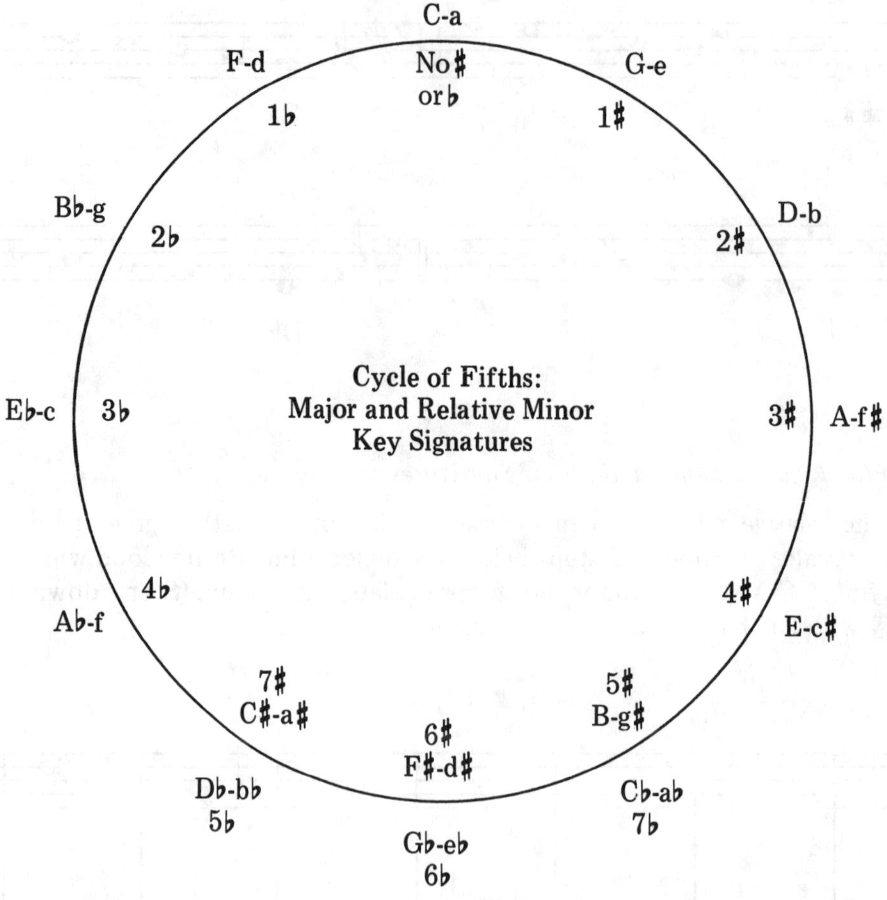

Alternate Keys

Just as there are pairs of enharmonic keys (p. 112), in which the pitch and keyboard track are identical but the key signature and notation are different, there are pairs which we could call "alternate keys," in which the notation is identical but the pitches, keyboard track, and key signature are different.

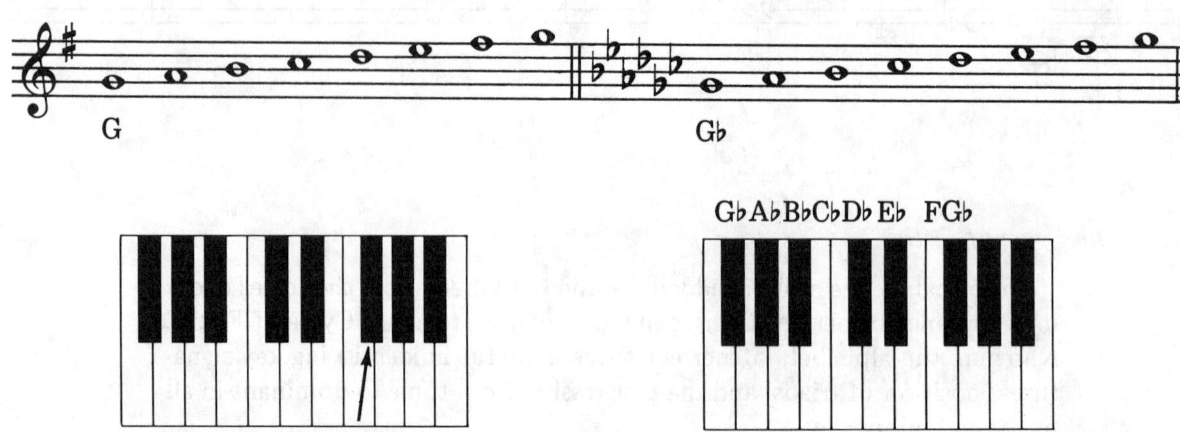

Learning the Major Scales

Two phases are involved in mastering the performance of scales: learning which keys to play, and how to finger them.

A clear visual image of the piano keys in a given scale can be acquired by depressing simultaneously the eight keys belonging to the complete scale. For fingering, the scale can be divided into two tetrachords of four keys each. Play the lower tetrachord as a cluster with the left hand, the upper tetrachord with the right hand. The G scale, shown in the keyboard diagram on page 114, would be played thus.

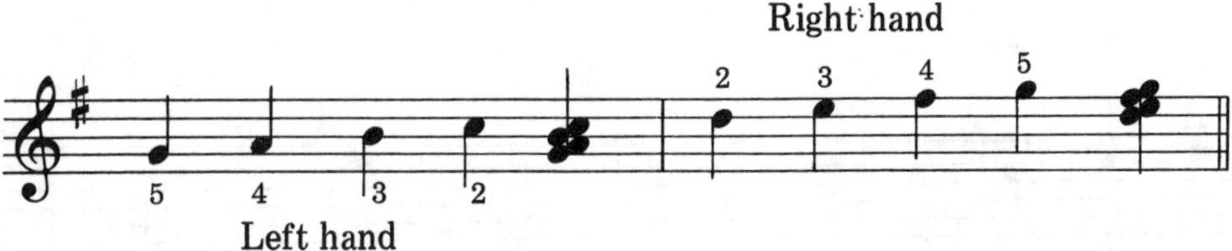

Memorize the keyboard track of the scale by thinking key color ("white, white," and so on) while recalling the image of the keys. Then test your memory by playing the scale up and down at least two octaves, each hand alone, using only the index finger.

TECHNIQUE

Finding Scale Fingerings

Although the musical activities in Unit Five involve only key signatures of up to two sharps or flats, the basic principles given here apply to fingering all scales.

Since there are eight different keys in each scale—the eighth being the same pitch as the first, an octave higher—some fingers must play more than one key within each octave. This change in hand position requires at least one thumb crossing. For easier playing, the thumb should play only white keys, and should never cross under another finger to a black key.

Every scale may be divided into groups of three and four keys for fingering purposes. This means that when a scale is played for two or more octaves, the crossings made by the thumb will alternate under fingers 3 and 4.

The fingering groups are most easily found by playing the scale up two octaves in the right hand and down two octaves in the left hand. When the tonic falls on a white key (as in the keys of C, G, D, and F), start with the thumb and make the first crossing under the third finger. This leaves four keys to be played before the thumb again plays the tonic; at this point, cross the thumb under the fourth finger. The final tonic may be played by the fifth finger.

C, G, D, right hand

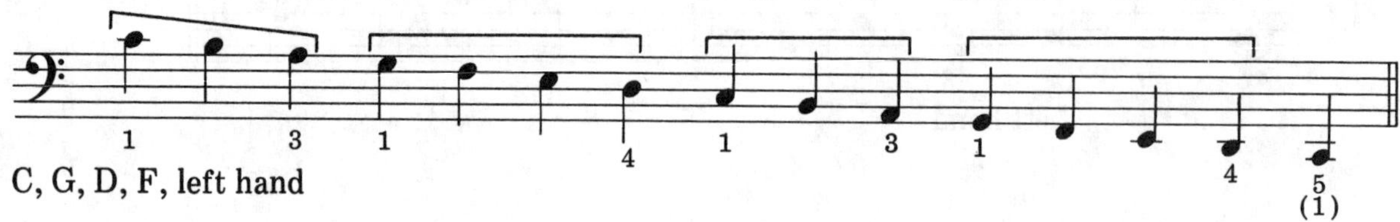

C, G, D, F, left hand

Exception: F in the right hand. The fourth degree is a black key; hence the thumb crosses under the fourth finger first, then under the third. The final tonic is played by the fourth finger.

F, right hand

Alternative choice for D, left hand: Because it is more comfortable to cross the thumb under when the third or fourth finger plays a black key, and to cross the third or fourth finger over the thumb to a black key, some pianists prefer the following fingering.

D, left hand

When the tonic falls on a black key (B♭), the thumb plays the first white key occurring in the scale and the white key immediately following the next black key.

B♭, right hand

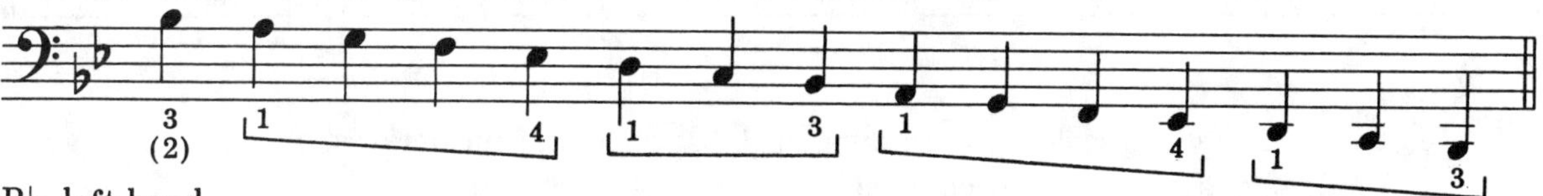

B♭, left hand

Memorizing Scale Fingerings

You can master the fingering of any scale more quickly and with fewer repetitions with the help of these four initial steps.

1. Play the scale up and down two octaves, in three- and four-note clusters. (Play the left hand one or two octaves lower.)

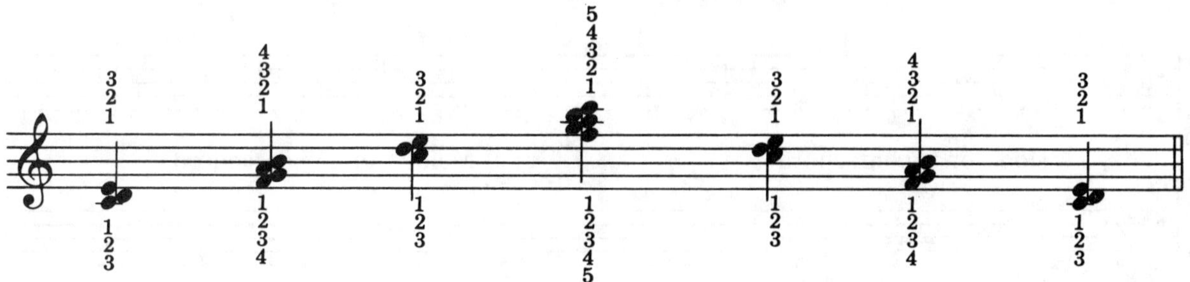

2. Play the right hand up two octaves in even quarter notes, followed by the left hand down. Repeat until you can play securely and fluently.

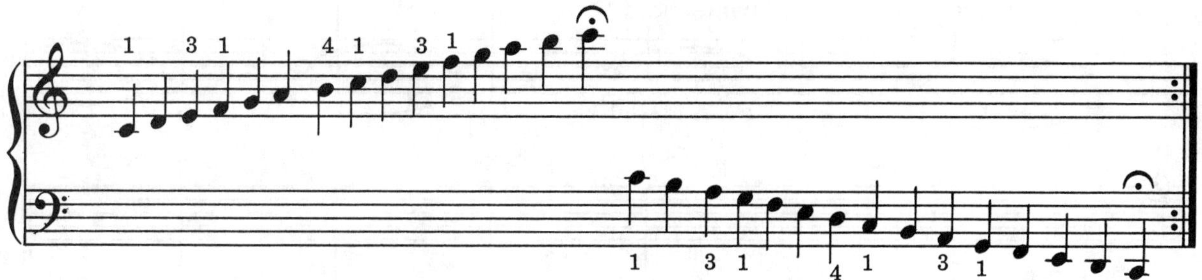

3. Play the right hand down in even quarter notes, followed by the left hand up. Concentrate on the choice of finger to cross, and locate firmly in mind which key is to be played by the fourth finger. Note that the fourth finger plays only one key within each octave, whereas the other fingers play two different ones.

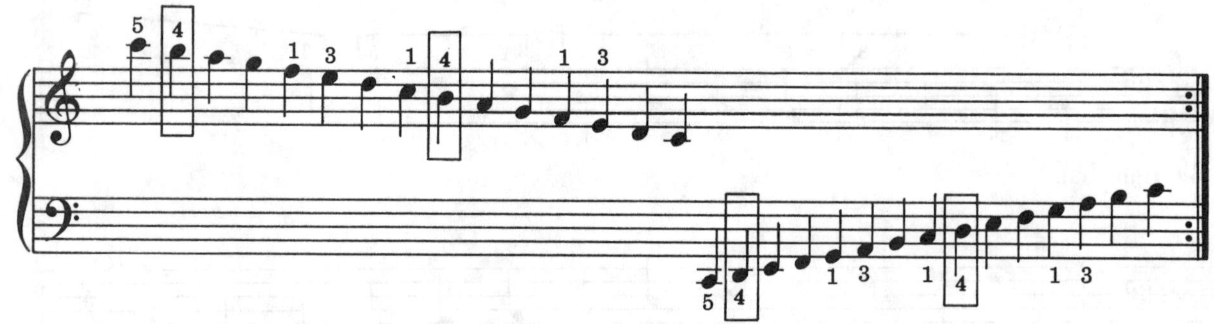

4. Play the scale up and down, each hand alone, four octaves, once in quarter notes, twice in eighth notes.

IMPROVISATION

Movement Throughout the Scale

1. Structure Accompaniment of perfect fifths up and down the scale
   Melody based on pentachords of each of the seven degrees up the scale
   Restriction: avoid the diminished fifth on the seventh degree
   Keys of C, G, D, F, and B♭

Melody on C pentachord

Melody on D pentachord

Improvise on E pentachord

Improvise on F pentachord

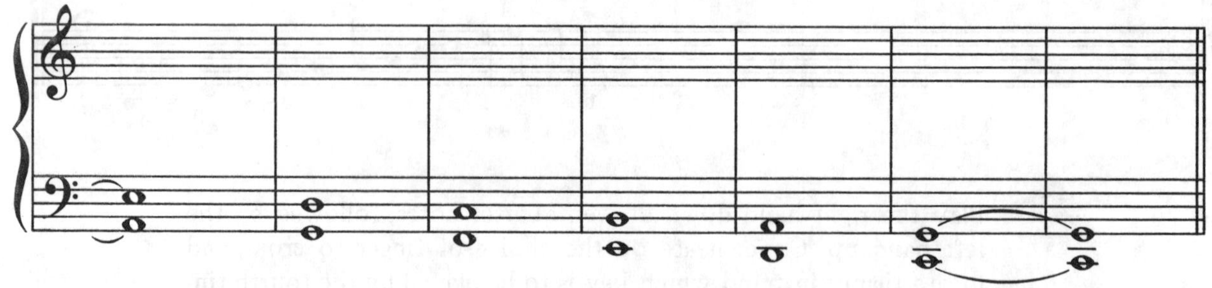

Transpose the accompaniment to G, F, D, and B♭, improvising melodies from the pentachords within those keys.

2. Structure Accompaniment of perfect fifths up and down the scale, omitting the diminished fifth on the second degree
Melody based on pentachords matching the fifths in the accompaniment
Aeolian mode on A, E, B, D, and G

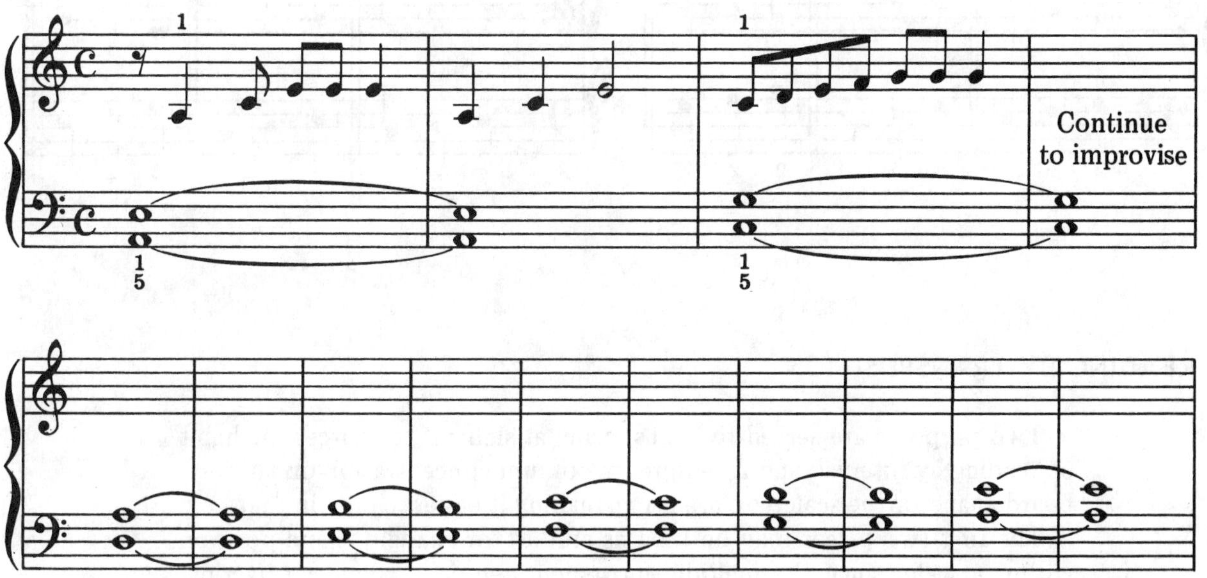

Variant: In the descending progression of fifths in the accompaniment, include a perfect fifth on the flatted second degree (B♭-F in the key of A).

TECHNIQUE

Single-Finger Scales for Security with Key Signatures

Play the G, D, F, and B♭ major scales and the E, B, D, and G natural minor scales two octaves up and down, hands-together, in parallel motion. Use a detached touch, using only the second finger of each hand. Play the sequence in the following ways.

1. Hands one octave apart
2. Hands a tenth apart, starting the left hand on the tonic
3. Hands a sixth apart, starting the right hand on the tonic

Example of starting positions in G and e.

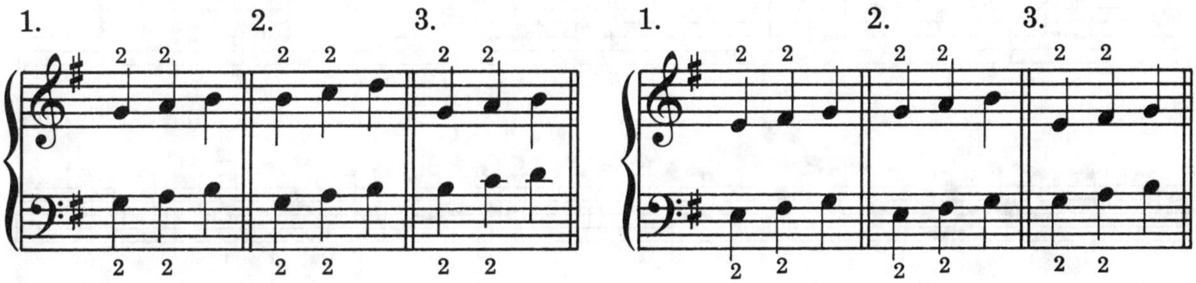

Play the same scales in the same manner in contrary motion from the following starting positions.

READING BY TRANSPOSITION

Two purposes are served by transposing at sight: it reinforces the habit of reading by interval, and it requires maximum concentration on the keyboard shape of the scale you are using, making it easier to play in that key.

The first two pieces may be used as studies for changing hand position within a scale, since the melodic movement requires irregular fingering. Try playing both in succession in the same key, starting with G and F, then going on to D and B♭. Use the same fingering for all keys. For most effective learning, it is best *not* to play the melodies in the key of C before transposing.

Selections 3-10 are notated in various keys. The given fingering is suitable for all keys except those indicated by an asterisk. When transposing into those keys, before playing, visualize mentally the keys to be played and plan a fingering that will avoid placing the thumb on a black key. (Exception: top of a wide skip, such as the seventh in 5.

7. C D *F B♭
England
8. C F D G
Schubert
9. F C G *B♭
Netherlands
10. G C F *B♭
England

Selections 11-12 are in Aeolian mode (natural minor).

11. e d g b

U. S.

12. a b g e

César Franck

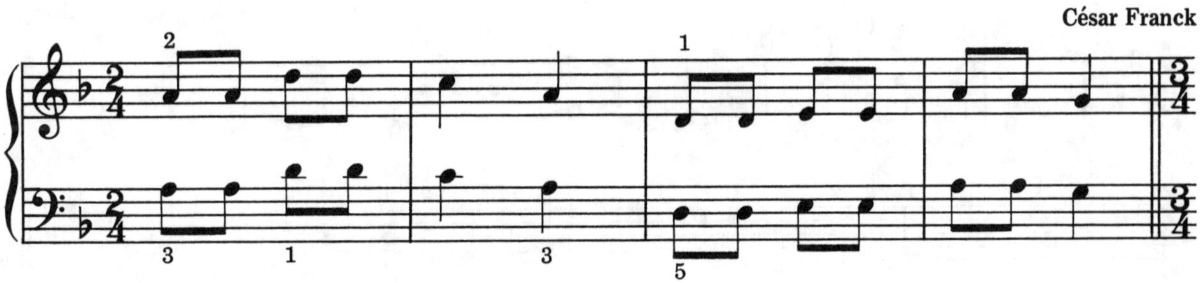

Selections 13-14 are based on the harmonic minor scale (see p. 71). The raised seventh degree is always indicated by an accidental in the score. In the keys of a, e, b, d, and g, this accidental will always be a sharp, and the key to be played will be black. (Selection 13 also includes the natural minor.)

Before reading in transposition, it is useful to play the harmonic minor scale up and down, single-finger fashion.

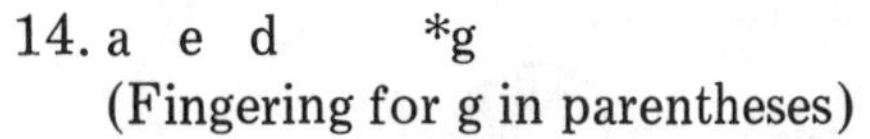

In 15, the seventh degree follows or leads to the tonic several times. (In such usage, the seventh is always raised.) One passage is based on the ascending melodic minor (see p. 73), in which the sixth as well as the seventh degree is raised a half step. In transposing to d and g, the progression from the sixth to the seventh degree will be from a white to a black key, differing from the keyboard pattern of the notated key and from a and b.

PLAYING BY EAR

Melody Only

Sing the melody of "When the Saints Go Marching In" from memory. Do not look at the notes or scan them before singing. Determine the mode and the pitch range of the melody. Identify the scale degree of the initial pitch.

One way to check your aural skill is to look at the keyboard while singing and follow the keyboard track of the melody. Play single keys at various points, such as at the word "in." If the key you play matches the note you sing, you have traced the melody correctly.

Sing the melody again, "playing" it on the closed fallboard of the piano or on your lap. The fingering should match the intervals you hear. Then play it in a key of your own choice, checking whether you identified the intervals correctly.

Transpose to other keys. You will probably find yourself recalling the fingering pattern or the intervallic movement, as well as the sound, while playing. You may also use analysis: "tonic, third, fourth, fifth degrees of the scale." These are all components of the memorization process.

Melody and Accompaniment, Using IV

Listen as your instructor plays the following arrangement for two hands of "When the Saints Go Marching In." Identify the scale position of each bass note by ear. Check your accuracy by scanning the score of what was played.

Play the complete arrangement by ear and memory. Notice the complementary rhythm pattern of the accompaniment. Transpose to other keys.

The accompaniment to "When the Saints Go Marching In" consists of single chord tones. In measures 1-10 and 13-16, the implied chord was either I or V. In measures 11 and 12, the fourth scale degree implies a chord based on that degree as the root.

This is the subdominant triad. The tonic, dominant, and subdominant are the principal triads upon which melodic and harmonic structures were based in Western music, until late-nineteenth- and early-twentieth-century composers introduced new concepts. Most traditional melodies can be harmonized with these three chords.

IMPROVISATION

Melody and Accompaniment in Twelve-Bar Blues Form

One use of IV is in the twelve-bar blues structure, which is characterized by the chord progression and rhythm of the accompaniment: I-IV-I-V-IV-I, always in the number of measures shown below.

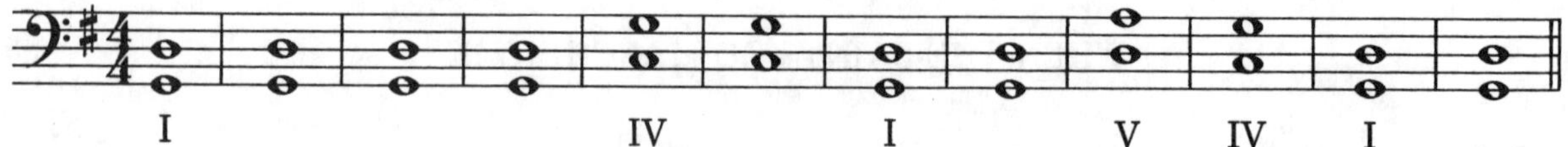

One-measure melodic patterns may be improvised on the bass. Often these patterns lie within the framework of the major triad.

It is characteristic of the blues melodic idiom to mix minor and major modes. An example of this occurs in the skeleton score given below. Complete the score by following the instructions below. Transpose to other keys.

BLUE SAINTS GO MARCHING

Improvise melodic patterns and play blues accompaniment in several keys.

HARMONIZATION

Duet Secondos by Ear

Your instructor or a class member will play the following primo parts while you play the secondo. Secondos may be based on perfect fifths, as indicated in the suggestions for rhythm and voicing below. Choice of I, IV, or V is to be made by ear. Each may be transposed to other keys.

The primo melodies are to be played hands-together an octave apart.

1. SHE'LL BE COMING ROUND THE MOUNTAIN

Primo

2. BATTLE HYMN OF THE REPUBLIC

Primo

Secondo

3. BILLY BOY

Primo

Harmonization with I, IV, and V

Each scale degree may be a member (root, third, fifth, or seventh) of at least one of the three principal chords, or *primary triads*, used for harmonization.

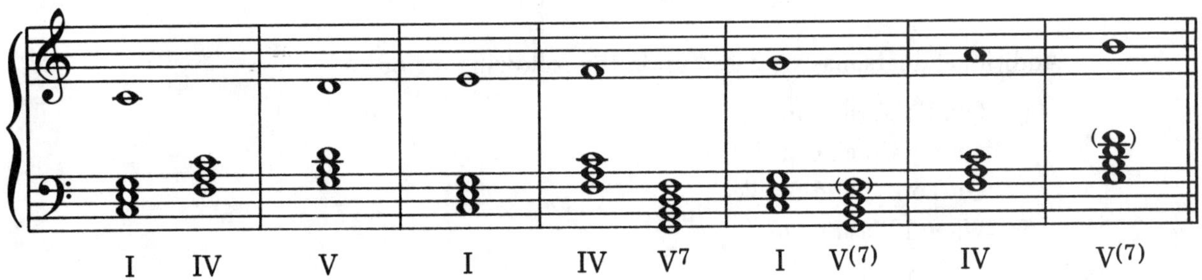

Chord progressions including the subdominant:

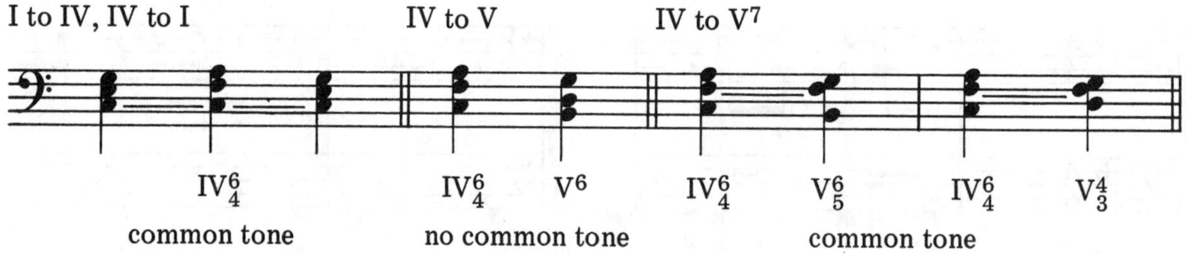

Duet Secondos Based on Close Progression of I, IV, and V

The primo of a duet is notated below. Complete the secondo by ear as the primo is played. Transpose to other keys.

The primo should be played hands-together an octave apart.

DU, DU LIEGST MIR IM HERZEN

Additional duets may be based upon the following melodies:

"Old Folks at Home"
"Jimmy Crack Corn"
"On Top of Old Smoky"
"When I Was Single"

For further experience in harmonizing by ear, accompany yourself on the piano as you sing or whistle the melodies.

TECHNIQUE

Chord Progressions

Practice these chord progressions in the keys of C, G, D, F, and B♭. Be sure to use the second finger in the left hand on IV.

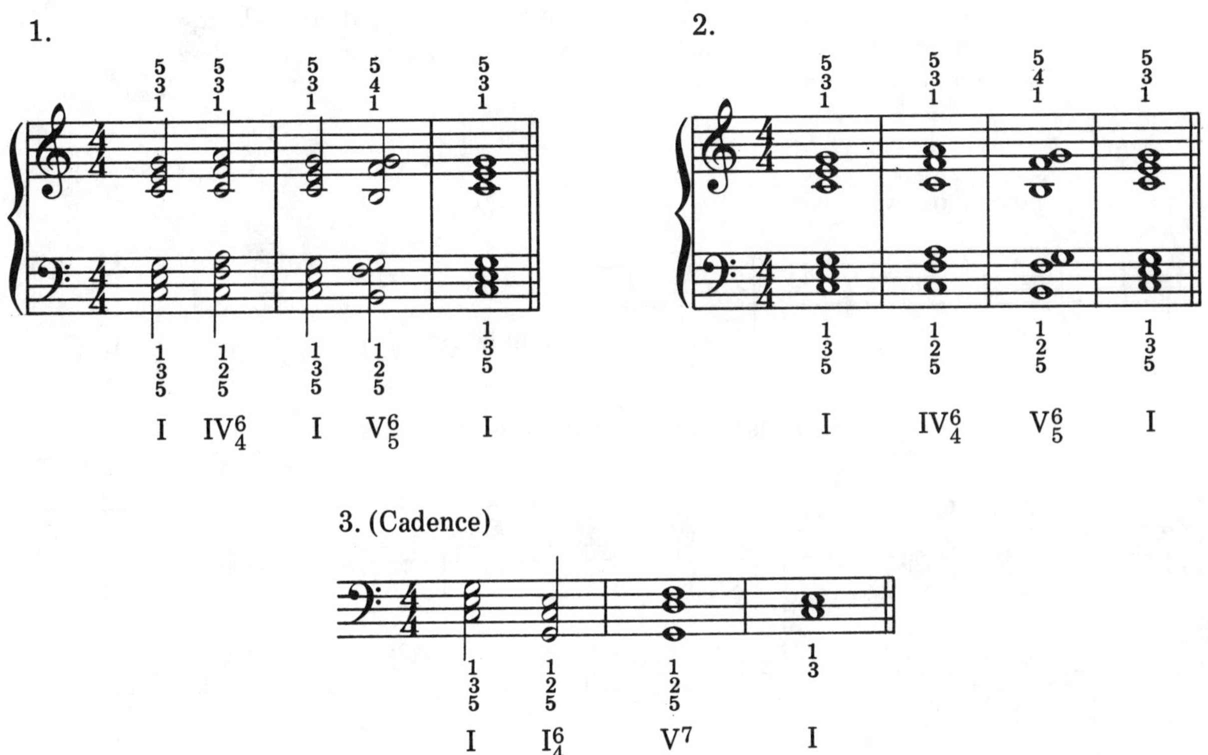

Primary and Secondary Triads in Root Position

Play triads up the scale, reciting aloud the Roman numeral, root name, and quality of each while playing. Transpose to G, D, F, and B♭.

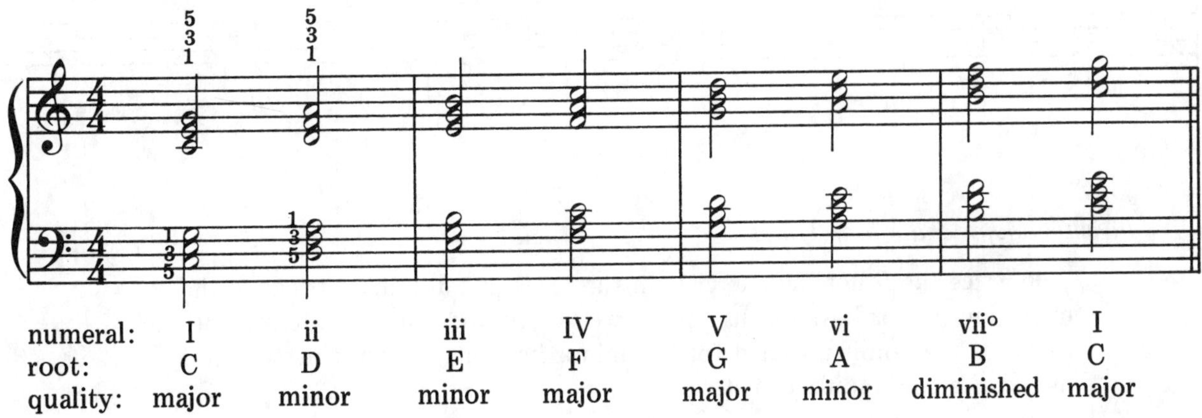

Major and Minor Triads

1. To strengthen your memory of major and minor triads, first memorize major thirds as keyboard shapes.

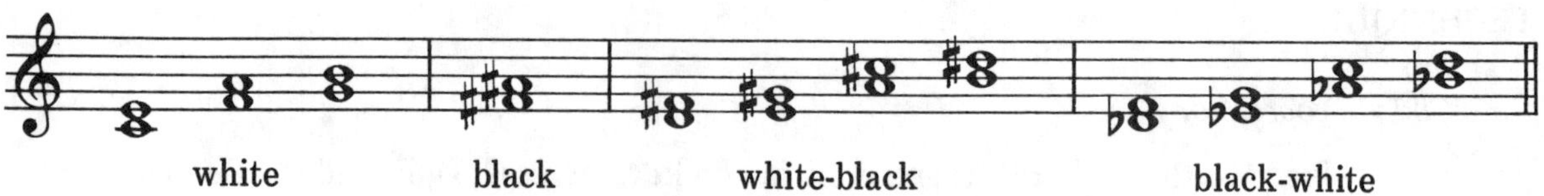

2. Memorize all major triads by playing the I chord of each key around the cycle of fifths. Play hands singly and together, using the pattern shown.

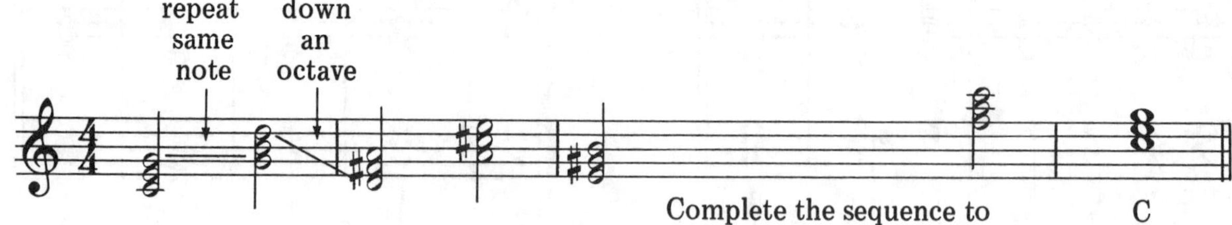

3. Change major triads to minor around the cycle of fifths.

4. Change major triads to minor in chromatic progression.

Inverted Major and Minor Triads

Practice the following exercise on the tonic and dominant triads of the major and minor keys having up to two sharps and two flats. Remember to make the dominant triad for the minor keys major, since most minor melodies are harmonized that way.

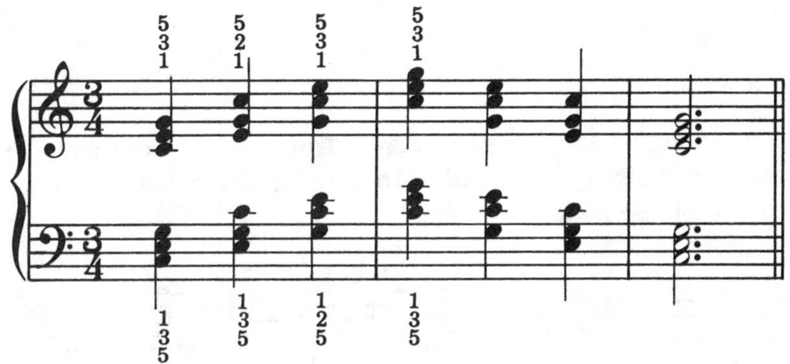

Close Progression of i, iv, V^7

Memorize the progression for the minor keys a, e, b, d, and g.

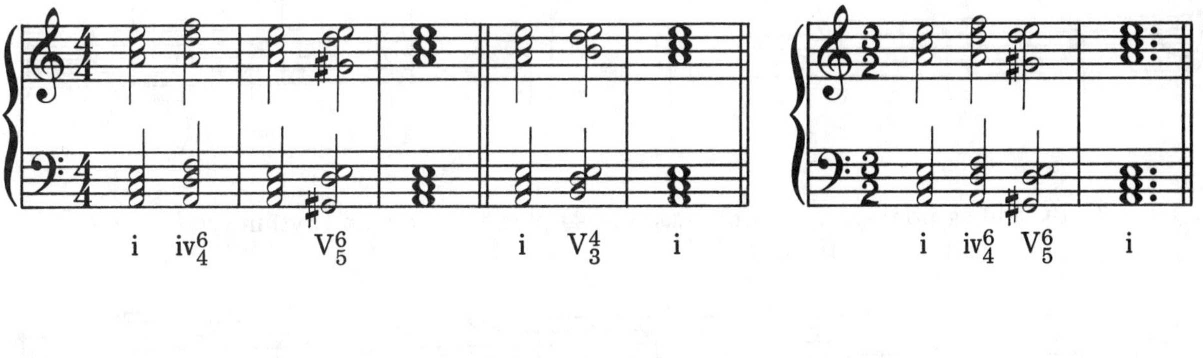

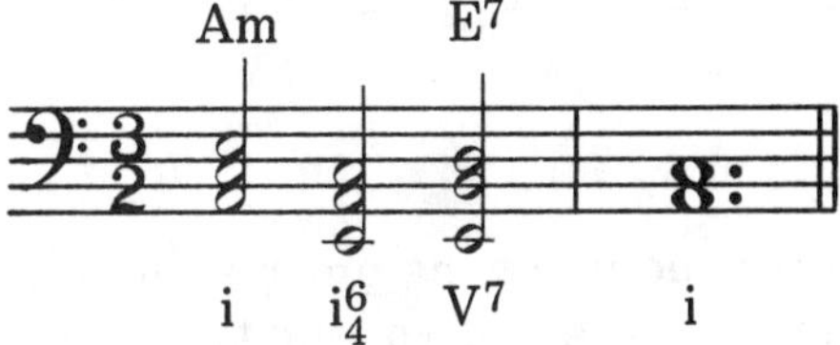

Three-Voiced V^7 in Root Position and Inversions

Knowing the hand positions for V^7 in first and second inversion is helpful if you must make a quick choice in harmonization (see also pp. 66-68). Memorize this progression for the major and minor keys having up to two sharps and two flats.

IMPROVISATION

Melodies to Given Chords

Since the ideas for many melodies grow from chords, your melodic inventiveness can grow by improvising to chords. Given below is a chord plan for a two-phrase period.

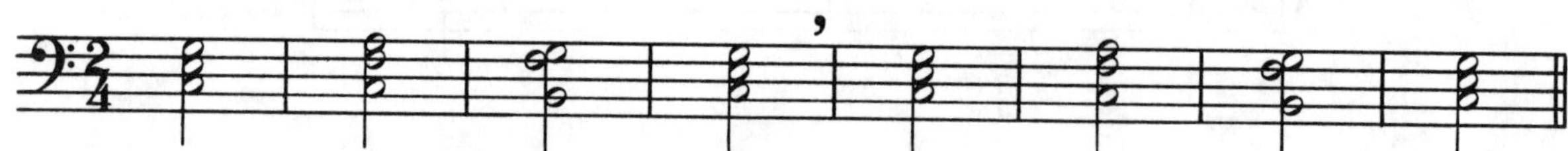

To begin with, select only chord members for the melody.

By adding nonharmonic tones (see p. 64) plus variations in rhythm, you can begin to enrich the melody.

Improvise melodies over the following progression in $\frac{2}{4}$, $\frac{3}{4}$, and $\frac{6}{8}$ meters. Play in the keys having up to two sharps and two flats. Use one chord per measure.

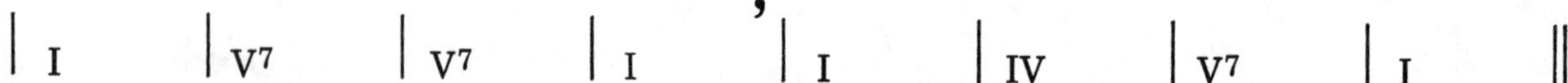

Improvise original chord progressions as a basis for melodic improvisation. Explore irregular phrase lengths of five, six, and seven measures.

PLAYING BY EAR

1. **Schubert, "Der Lindenbaum"**
   Given below is the harmonic analysis of this Schubert song. Your instructor or a class member should play the melody. As you hear it, play an accompaniment of a blocked chord on the first beat of each measure.

In the two measures where a change takes place, it is on the third beat.

Key of F

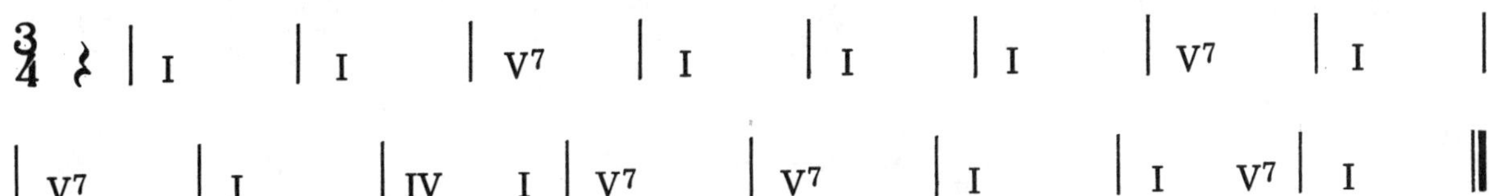

When the melody has become familiar, play it by ear, adding an accompaniment when ready.

Suggested accompaniment pattern

DER LINDENBAUM

2. Brahms, "Wiegenlied"
   Proceed as with 1.

   Key of D

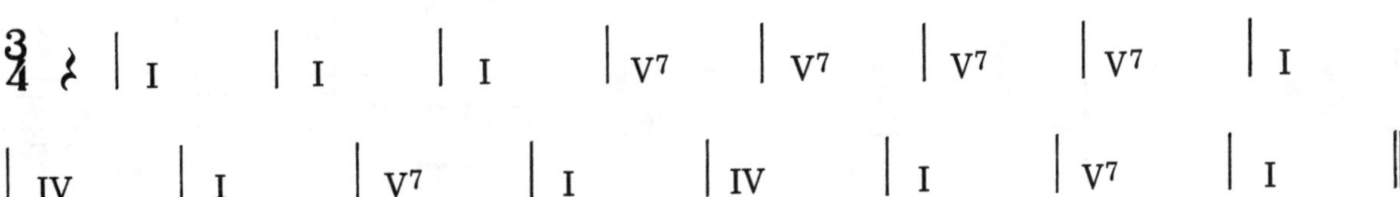

Suggested accompaniment pattern

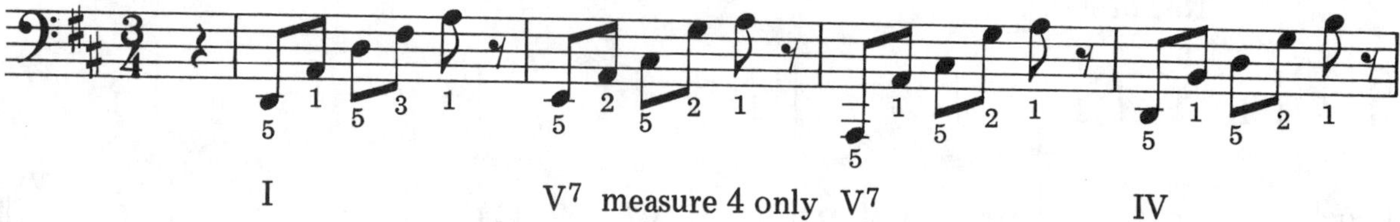

WIEGENLIED

IMPROVISATION

Accompaniments to Notated Melodies

Roman numerals I, IV, V indicate choice of chords; choice of position is the option of the performer. When V is given, either a triad or a seventh chord is acceptable.

Suggested accompaniment patterns are given with each melody. It is also acceptable simply to employ the close chord progression, playing a chord on the downbeat of each measure.

1. THIS OLD MAN

1
I
V
I

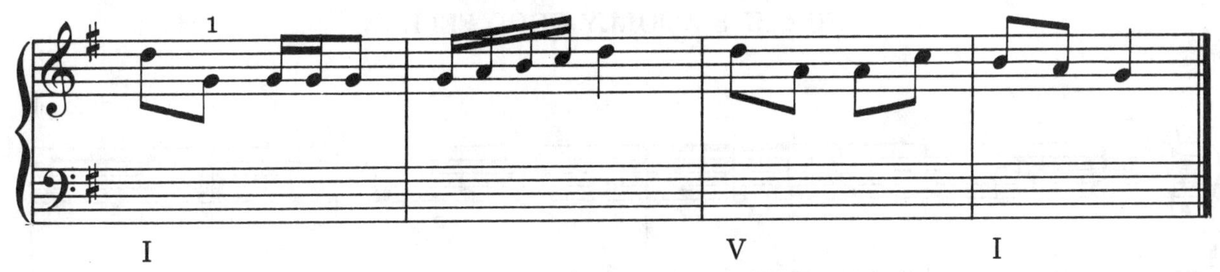

2. MARINES' HYMN

U. S.

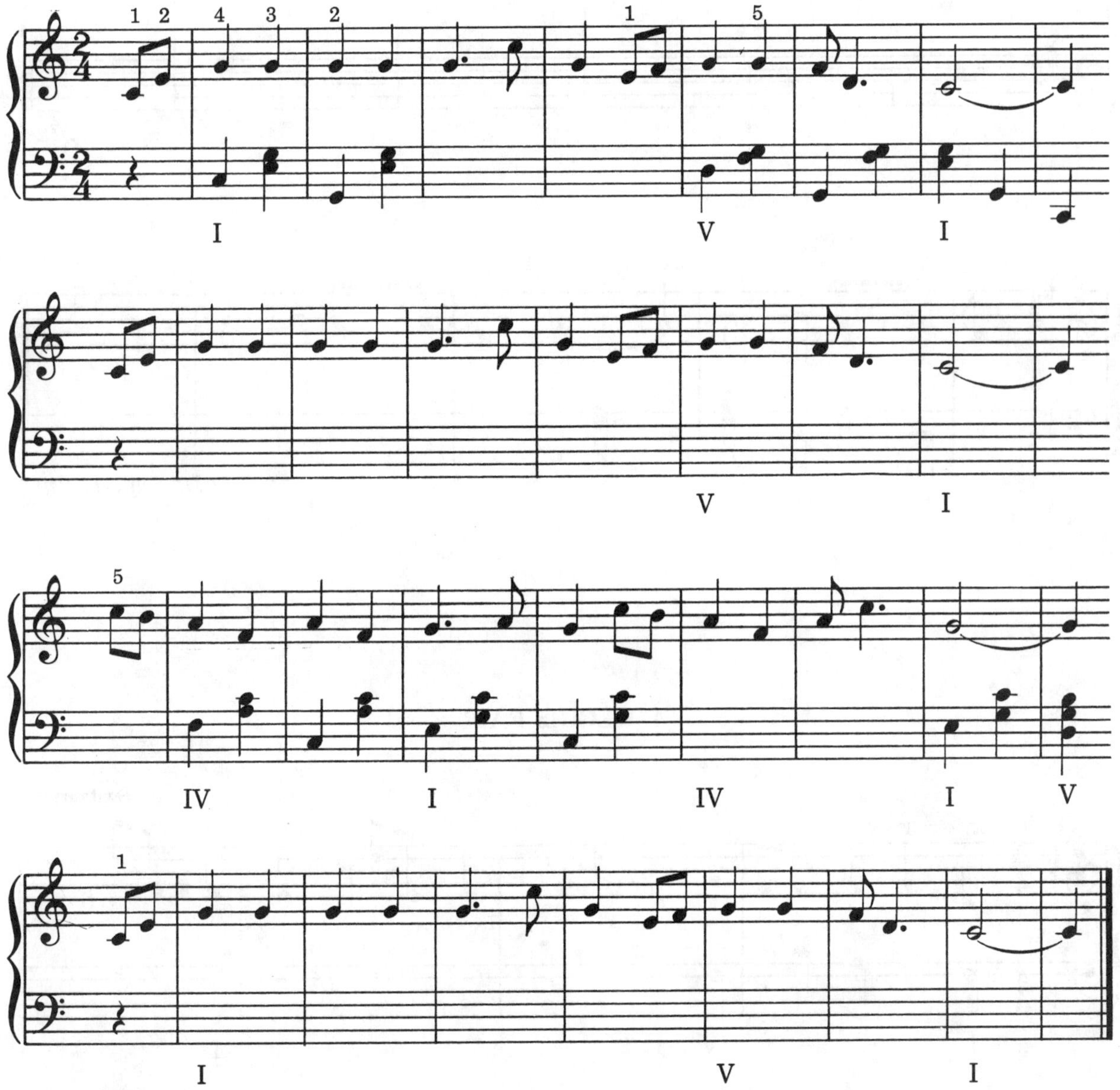
1 2
4
3
2
1
5
I
V
I
V
I
5
IV
I
IV
I
V
1
I
V
I

3. FOR HE'S A JOLLY GOOD FELLOW

Traditional

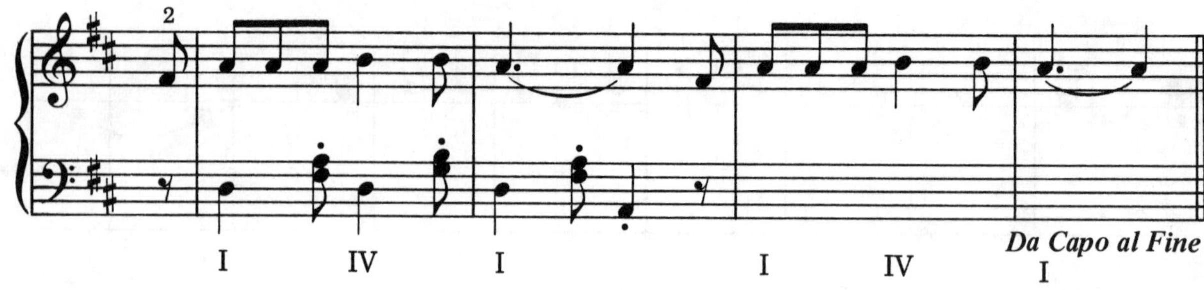

4. WEGGIS FAIR

Switzerland

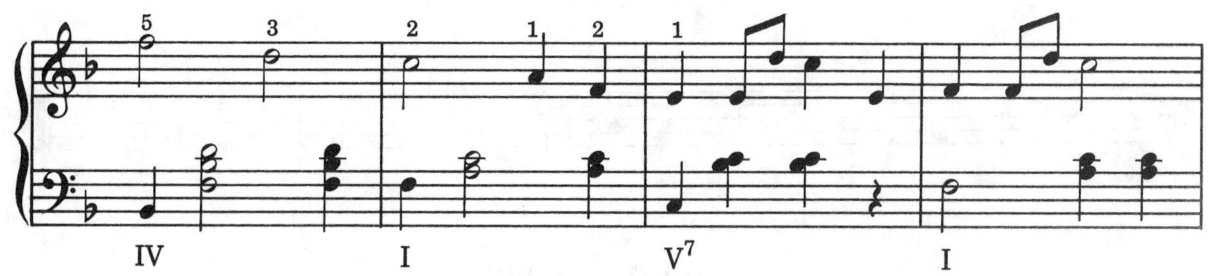

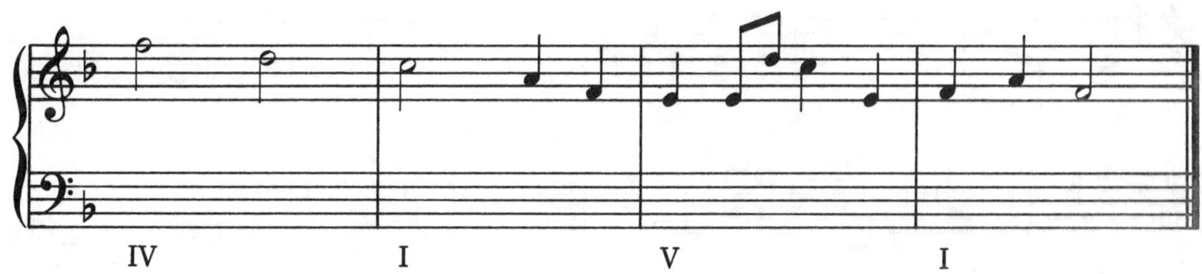

HARMONIZATION

By Ear, Without Roman Numerals

1. CRADLE SONG

2. LI'L LIZA JANE

3. GET ON BOARD

4. RING THE BANJO

Chord Symbols

In many publications, chords suitable for harmonization of melodies are indicated by letters placed above the staff, generally referred to as *chord symbols.* A letter alone (C) indicates a major triad; a letter accompanied by a 7 (G^7) indicates a dominant seventh chord (V^7 or major-minor seventh). The performer may choose any position and voicing.

In the following two melodies, both chord symbols and Roman numerals are given. For transposition, use the numerals as a guide.

5. DOWN IN THE VALLEY

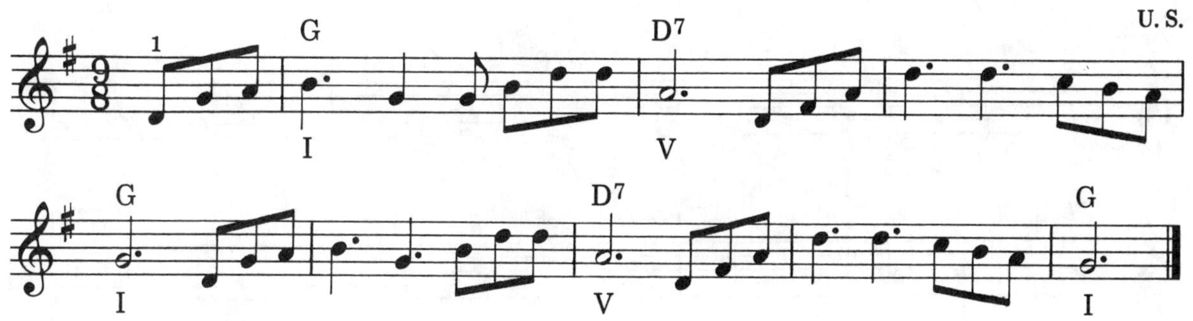

6. GO IN AND OUT THE WINDOW

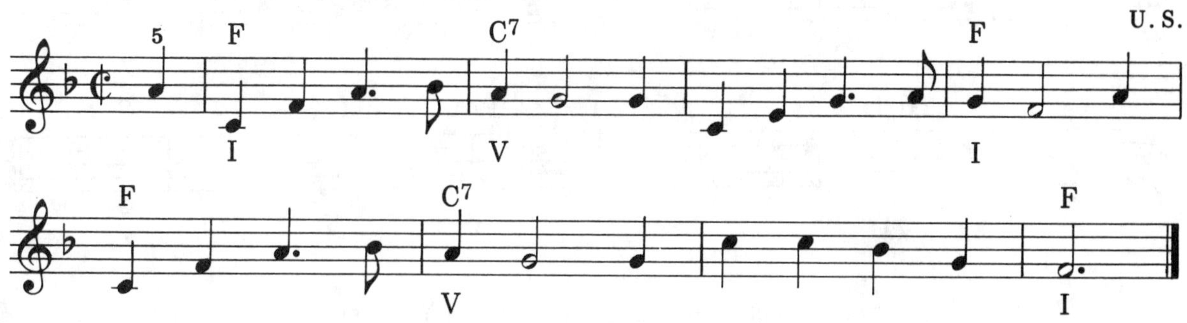

In the following melody, only chord symbols are given. Melody and accompaniment should be transposed to other keys; mentally supply the Roman numerals to do this.

7. THE MUFFIN MAN

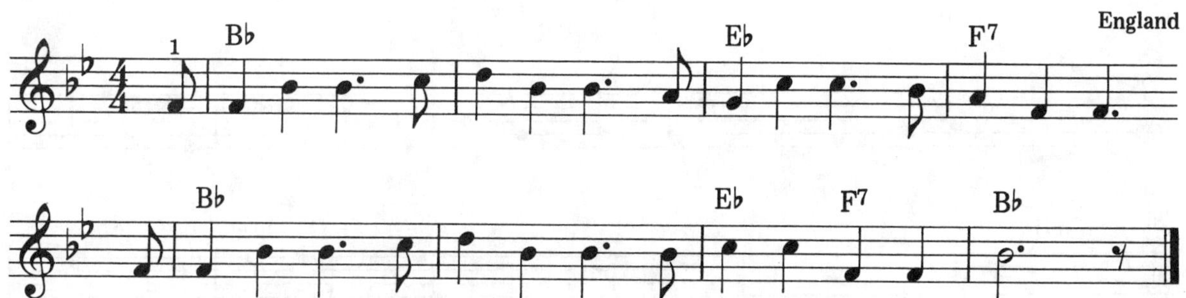

In chord-symbol usage, specific chord positions may be indicated by adding the letter name of the note to be played in the bass. For example, F/C means that C is to be played in the bass.

Specific positions are suggested for the following melody, both by chord symbols and the Roman numerals.

8. OLD BLACK JOE

For the following melodies, only chord symbols are given. For transposition, mentally supply the Roman numerals.

9. YANKEE DOODLE

10. MARY'S LULLABY

UNIT SIX

Playing in Modes Other than Major and Minor

HARMONIZATION

In Aeolian Mode

Melodies in modes other than harmonic minor may also be harmonized with triads in root position. In natural minor (Aeolian mode), the three primary triads, i, iv, and v, are all minor.

These triads usually provide a satisfactory harmony, as notated in the score of "Wraggle Taggle Gypsies." The secondary triads provide additional color. Two optional chord progressions that include secondary triads are indicated below the score.

1. WRAGGLE TAGGLE GYPSIES

Harmonize the three following melodies with triads of your own choice.

2. HIGH BARBARY

3. BLOW THE CANDLES OUT

Taken from *The New Song Fest,* ed. Dick and Beth Best.
Copyright 1948, 1955 by R. L. Best. Used by permission of Crown Publishers, Inc.

4. JOHNNY HAS GONE FOR A SOLDIER

U. S.

Transpose these Aeolian melodies and the harmonizations to other keys.

In Harmonic Minor

Use i, iv, and V^7 to harmonize the following melodies. Transpose to minor keys having up to two sharps and two flats.

1.

Spiritual

2. France

(See p. 204 for Tchaikovsky's piano solo arrangement of this melody.)

3. Hungary

(See p. 201 for Bartók's solo arrangement of this melody.)

4. Hungary

(See p. 200 for Bartók's solo arrangement of this melody.)

The following melody by Franz Schubert is in melodic minor. Schubert's harmonization is indicated for the first phrase of each period.

The rhythm notation is typical of vocal music, in which the choice of putting individual stems or connected beams on the notes depends upon the vocal syllabication. The pianist reading a vocal melody must supply his or her own fingering, which should be legato.

5. GUTE NACHT (EXCERPT)

Relative Major and Minor

In music from the Baroque through the Romantic era, major and minor are the only two modes encountered frequently. It is useful to be able to spot quickly whether a composition is in the major or the minor key associated with its key signature.

In traditional harmony, the consistent presence of an accidental may be a clue—it is likely to be the raised seventh degree of the harmonic minor (for example, g♯ in a piece with no sharps or flats). To identify the mode of a melody, besides checking the final note, which is often the tonic, you can scan the opening passage for the strong accents. These may fall on melody notes that are members of the tonic triad, major or minor.

In the three fragments below, the mode of each emerges within the first three measures.

Below is the melody of "Armes Waisenkind" by Robert Schumann, harmonized with i, iv, and V^7.

As shown in the following version, Schumann *modulated*, or changed key, from a to its relative major, and then returned to a, using an inverted secondary triad (vii^o_6) as a transitional chord back to the V^7 of a. The following score gives Schumann's harmonic progression in blocked chords. (See p. 202 for the complete composition with Schumann's fine voicing.) The modulation is indicated by the name of the new key before the modulatory chord (for example, C V^7 in measure 2). The harmony continues in that key until a new key is indicated. In measure 3, the vii^o_6 of C is also the ii^o_6 of a.

The following melody modulates three times, indicated by X's. Harmonize and transpose it to other minor keys.

WE THREE KINGS OF ORIENT ARE

John Hopkins

Identify by ear the two modulations in this melody.

EVERY TIME I FEEL THE SPIRIT

Spiritual

ii^6 As a Substitute for IV^6_4 at a Cadence

The secondary triad ii^6 is often substituted for a IV^6_4 in a final cadence because it makes a very strong ending. The first inversion is used because the bass line then moves from the fourth degree of the scale to the fifth. When a I^6 precedes the ii^6, as in the second ending of "Austrian Folk Melody," the ending becomes even more effective.

In this selection, the harmonization using I, IV^6_4, V^7 is given for the first period. The second ending gives the alternate harmonization, using ii^6, V^7, i. Harmonize the second period, using ii^6 where appropriate.

AUSTRIAN FOLK MELODY

Mozart used a ii^6 in his accompaniment to the following piece. Harmonize and transpose melody and accompaniment.

MINUET (EXCERPT)

W. A. Mozart

Write in the Roman numerals for the following piece. Note that Paisiello used all three positions of I, approaching ii^6 from I^6. Also note that he used a I^6_4 following the second occurrence of ii^6.

THE MILLER

Paisiello

Melodies to Harmonize with ii^6

Transpose melody and accompaniment to keys with up to two sharps or flats. (In chord-symbol usage, *m* indicates a minor triad.)

1. O SUSANNA

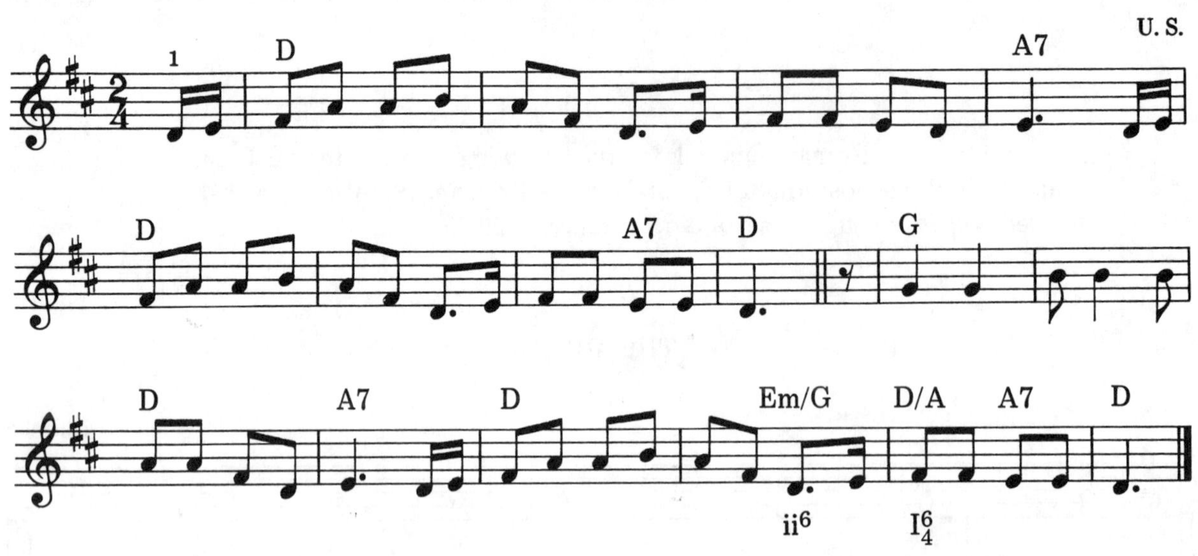

2. VIVE L'AMOUR

3. O TANNENBAUM

4. OLD BRASS WAGON

TECHNIQUE

Chord Progressions with ii^6

Memorize the following chord progressions in the keys of C, G, D, F, and B♭.

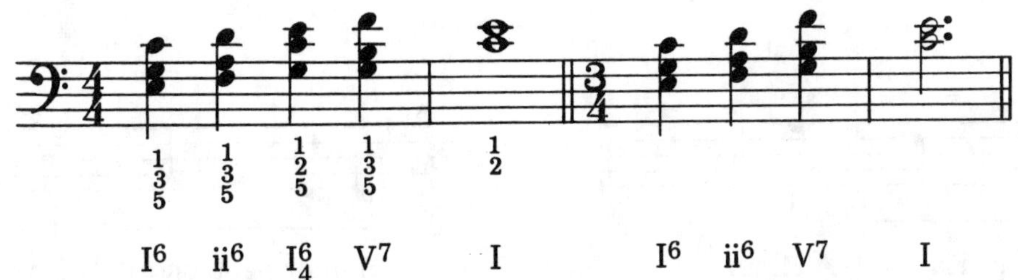

Classification of Modes Other than Major and Minor

Seven different modal scales may be found by playing up an octave, stepwise on the white keys, from each of the seven white keys starting with C. Each scale has a characteristic sound, which is determined by the order of whole and half steps, as shown below.

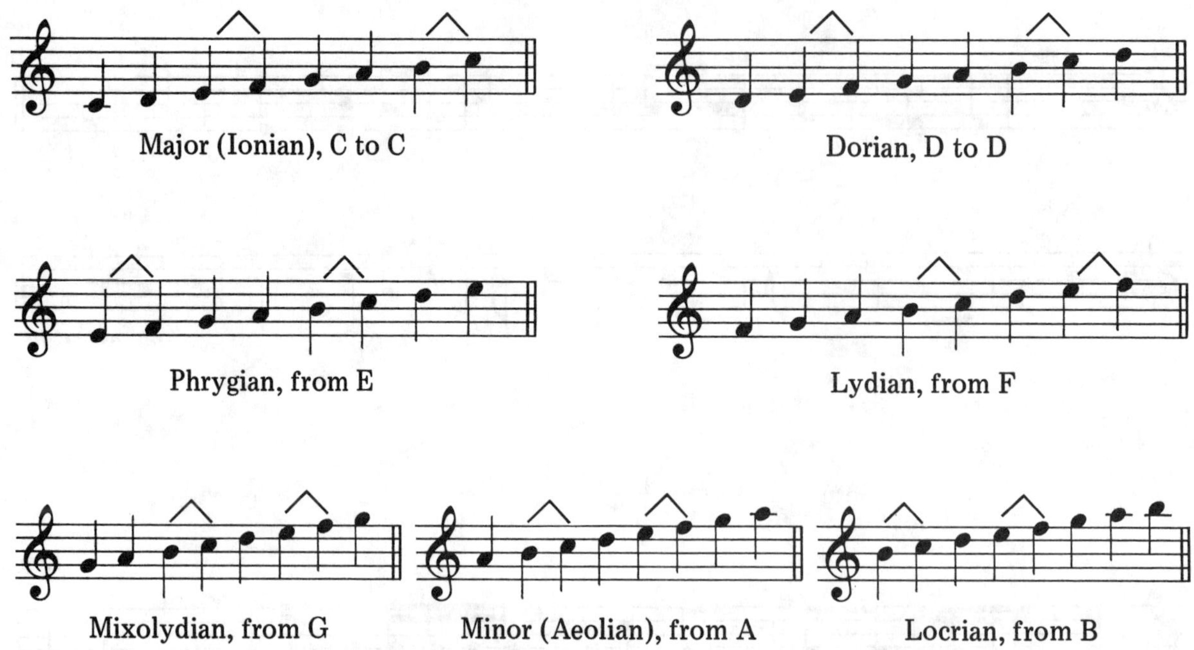

Major (Ionian), C to C

Dorian, D to D

Phrygian, from E

Lydian, from F

Mixolydian, from G

Minor (Aeolian), from A

Locrian, from B

Note: The earlier, or lower, in the scale the half steps occur, the "darker" the aural color of the mode.

Five of these modes have already been introduced in pentachords: major (Ionian), Phrygian, Lydian, minor (Aeolian), and Locrian (see pp. 28, 52, and 79). The remaining two, Mixolydian and Dorian, have a major or minor structure in the first five tones, but the location of the half step within the remaining three tones (counting the upper tonic as the eighth) is different from that of the major and minor scales.

major pentachord, C Major

major pentachord, G Mixolydian

minor pentachord, A Minor

minor pentachord, D Dorian

In three of the modes, the third degree of the scale is a major third above tonic; hence the tonic triad for each is major.

C Major F Lydian G Mixolydian

In three of the modes, the third degree of the scale is a minor third above tonic; hence the tonic triad for each is minor.

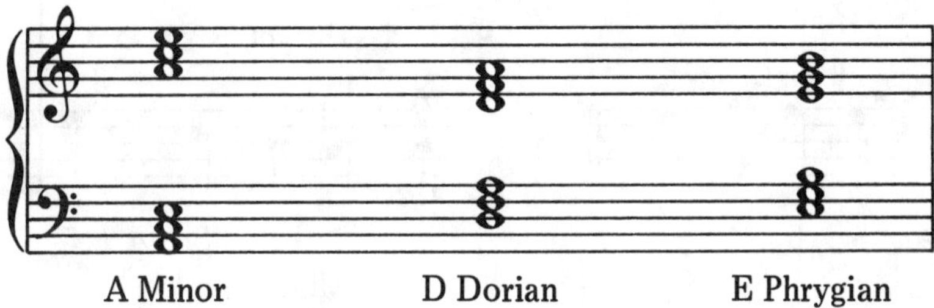

A Minor D Dorian E Phrygian

In the seventh mode, Locrian, the tonic triad is diminished.

B Locrian

The characteristic sounds of all modes except major (Ionian) and minor (Aeolian) may not be recognizable to you. To acquire familiarity with each mode and to be able to identify it by sound, classify each one as either major or minor according to the kind of tonic chord it has, and then identify the scale tone that deviates from the major or minor (circled in the following diagrams). The Lydian, Mixolydian, Phrygian, and Dorian modes have been transposed from their white-key positions so that their sounds can be compared with C major and A minor. (Since its tonic triad is diminished, the Locrian mode is rarely used by composers.)

Modes with a Major Tonic Triad

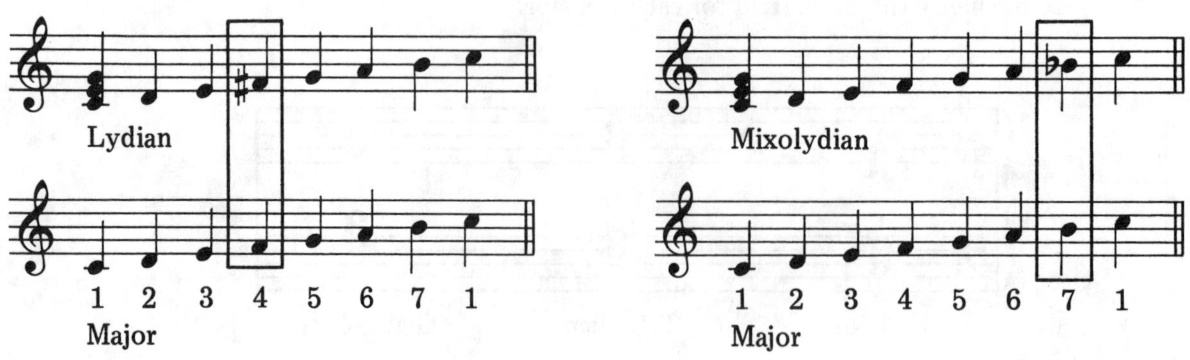

Modes with a Minor Tonic Triad

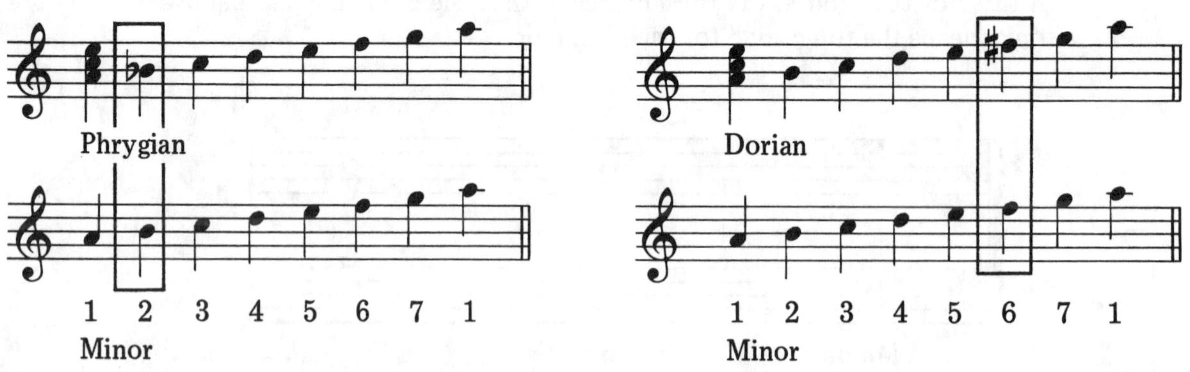

PLAYING BY EAR

Play and harmonize "What Shall We Do with the Drunken Sailor?" following these steps.

1. Sing "What Shall We Do with the Drunken Sailor?"
2. Sing the scale on which the melody is based. Identify the mode of the scale.
3. Find the scale of that mode on D, G, A, C, and E.
4. Play the melody in each of those tonalities.
5. Add an accompaniment of root-position triads or open fifths.

WHAT SHALL WE DO WITH THE DRUNKEN SAILOR?

U. S.

Key Signatures Applied to Modes

Key signatures of the major and minor tonalities are also used for music in the five other modes, and can be related to the signatures of the major and minor tonalities based on the same tonal center.

The Lydian mode sounds like major, but has a sharped fourth degree; hence the key signature will have one more sharp or one less flat than the major scale with the same tonic.

Examples

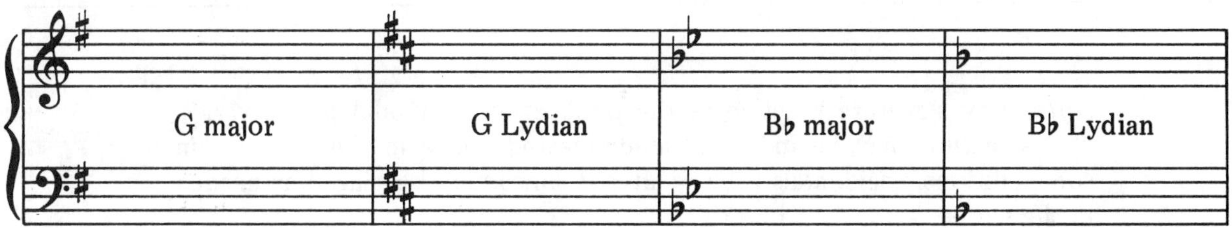

The Mixolydian mode sounds like major, but has a flatted seventh degree; hence it will have one more *flat* or one less *sharp* than the corresponding major.

Examples

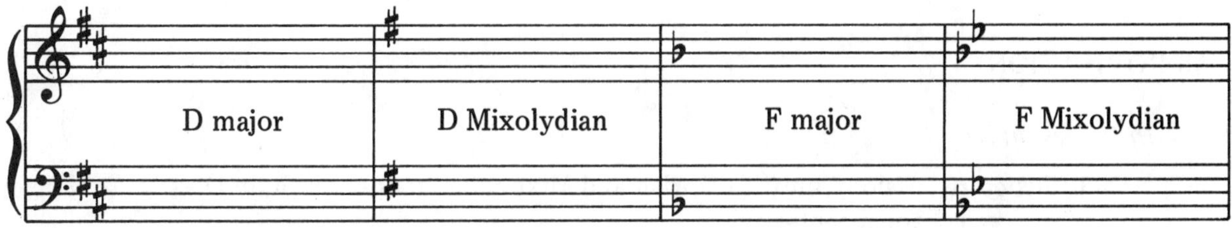

The Phrygian mode sounds like minor with a flatted second degree; hence it will have one more flat or one less sharp than the corresponding minor.

Examples

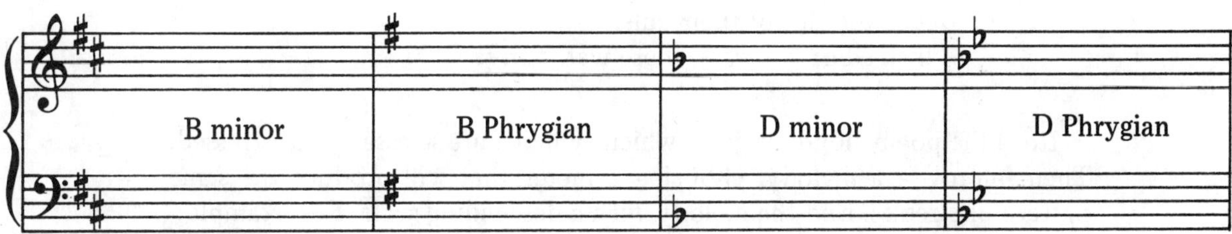

The Dorian mode sounds like minor with a sharped sixth degree; hence it will have one more sharp or one less flat than the corresponding minor.

Examples

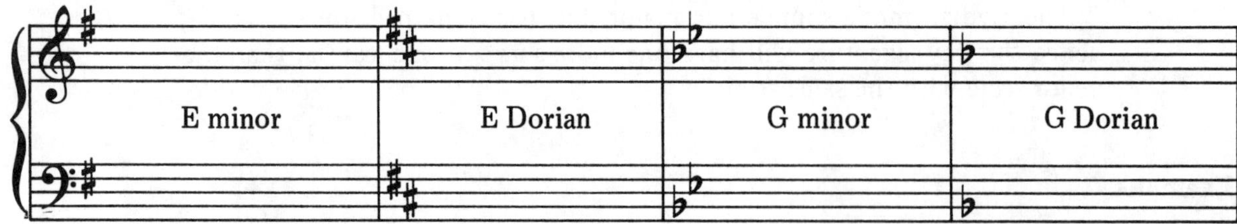

Note: Key signature practice in the publication of modal pieces varies. The signature may be indicated as delineated above in the text, or, in some editions, accidentals for the altered tones may be placed as needed in the score.

Examples

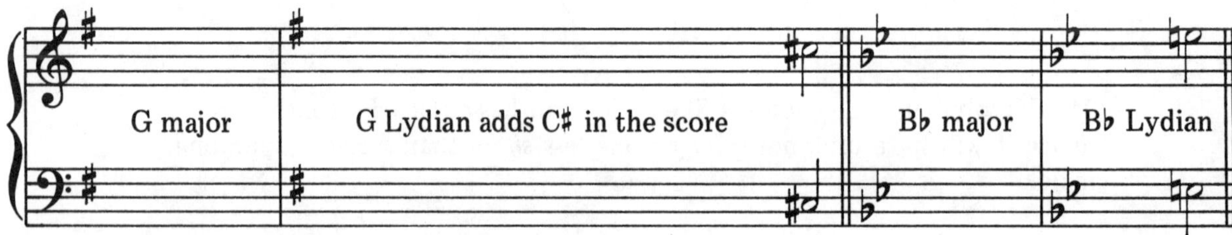

IMPROVISATION

In Modes on D

1. **Structure** Melody only, in Dorian and Mixolydian modes, each on D as tonal center
Rhythm and meter of "Kilkenny Cats"

Kilkenny Cats

(*Anonymous*)

There wanst was two cats of Kilkenny,
Each thought there was one cat too many,
So they quarreled and they fit,
They scratch'd and they bit,
Till, barrin' their nails,
And the tips of their tails,
Instead of two cats, there warnt any.

Read the poem aloud, noticing which syllables are stressed or unstressed. Then improvise a melody, choosing a meter that will produce the same pattern of stresses. End the melody with a descending scale. For example:

Dorian

Mixolydian

2. Structure Melody based on "Ring Out, Wild Bells." First stanza in Phrygian mode, second stanza in Lydian mode, both on D
Accompaniment of open fifths

Ring Out, Wild Bells

Alfred, Lord Tennyson

Ring out, wild bells, to the wild sky,
  The flying cloud, the frosty light:
  The year is dying in the night;
Ring out, wild bells, and let him die.

Ring out the old, ring in the new,
  Ring, happy bells, across the snow:
  The year is going, let him go;
Ring out the false, ring in the true.

Proceed as in improvisation 1. Each stanza may end with a descending scale.

First stanza in Phrygian mode

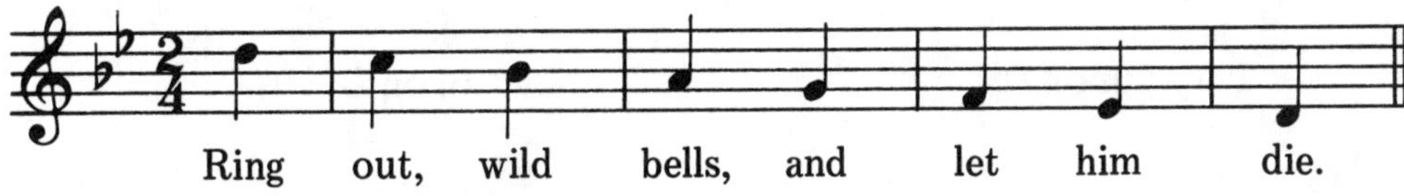

Second stanza in Lydian mode

HARMONIZATION

For Enhancement of Modal Character

In addition to the tonic triad (or an open fifth on the tonic), two other triads may be used as principal chords for each mode. These are major or minor triads in which one member is the characteristic tone of the mode.

In the Dorian mode, the sixth tone establishes the peculiar quality of the mode; hence, the triads in which that tone occurs will maintain the modal sound. In the Mixolydian mode, the seventh tone is the characteristic one. (Roman numerals indicate the positions of the chords in the modal scale.)

1. Accompaniment in Dorian and Mixolydian Modes

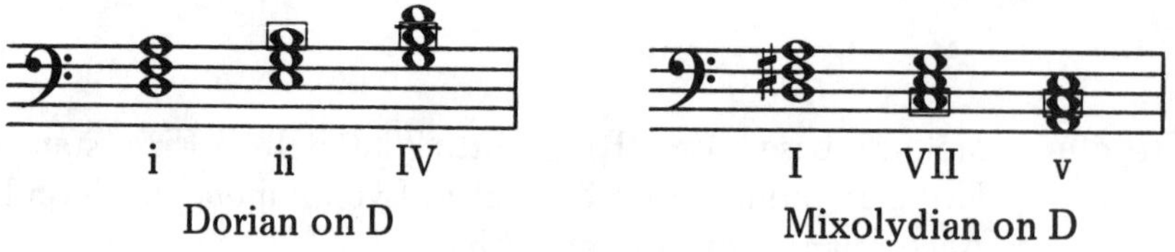

Suggested accompaniment for "Kilkenny Cats" (p. 160): ostinato of principal chords.

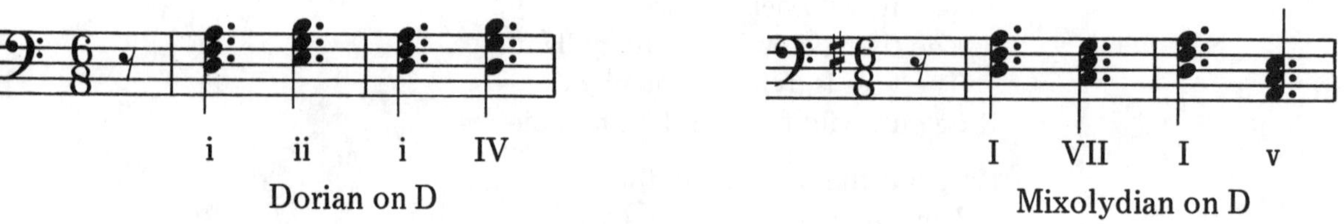

2. Accompaniment in Phrygian and Lydian Modes

In the Phrygian mode, the characteristic tone is the second degree; in the Lydian, it is the fourth. These tones occur in the following chords.

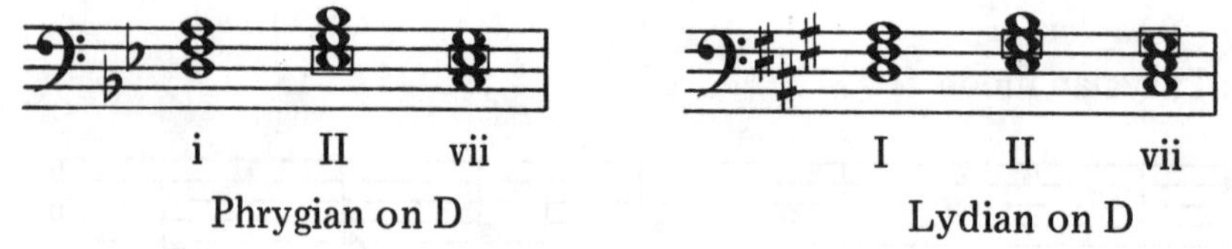

Suggested accompaniment patterns for "Ring Out, Wild Bells" (p. 161): ostinato of open fifths.

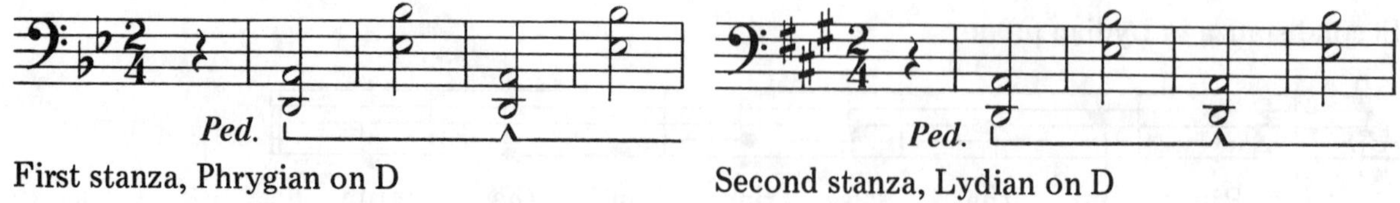

First stanza, Phrygian on D

Second stanza, Lydian on D

Modal Melodies to Harmonize

Identify the mode of each melody. Improvise a suitable accompaniment, using root-position triads or open fifths. Transpose to other keys.

In the suggested choice of chords or fifths for harmonization in "Jig Tune," note the inclusion of chords other than the principal ones.

1. JIG TUNE

2. HAUL AWAY, JOE

Lois Choksy, *The Kodaly Method: Comprehensive Music Education from Infant to Adult,* © 1974, No. 153. Adapted by L. G. by permission of Prentice-Hall, Inc., Englewood Cliffs, New Jersey.

In selections 3-4, the key signature for the corresponding minor or major key is used, with the altered tone for the mode indicated by an accidental in the score.

3. SCARBOROUGH FAIR

England

4. GREENSLEEVES

England

UNIT SEVEN

Reading and Repertoire in Ten Keys

This unit contains sight-reading and repertoire materials for more practice with the keys presented in Units Five and Six—the major and minor keys with up to two sharps or flats in the key signature. Once you have become familiar with the keyboard tracks of those keys, use the sight-reading exercises to help you recall them as you keep your eyes on the score.

TECHNIQUE

Keyboard Topography of Different Tonalities

The following exercises are useful as preparation for sight reading. They should be practiced in the key of the selection to be read until ease and fluency are attained without looking at the keys.

1.

Continue descending sequence back to C

2.

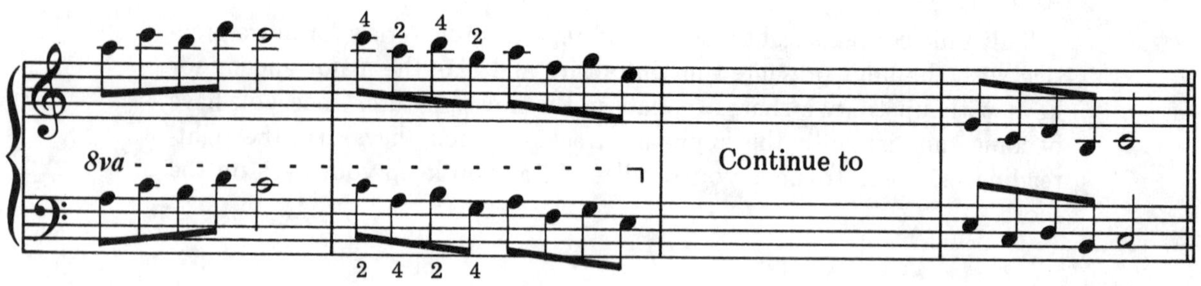

SIGHT READING

One Hand at a Time

Selection 1 may be performed as a duet or a solo. As a duet, the lower staff becomes the secondo, to be played by both hands; notes with stems down by the left hand, stems up by the right. The upper staff becomes the primo, to be played hands-together; the left hand as notated, using the fingering given below the notes; the right hand one octave higher, using the fingering above the notes.

As a solo, it is played exactly as notated. The best fingering for the left hand is 5-2-1 for each measure, except measure 8, in which it is 1-2-3.

1. HOME ON THE RANGE

U. S.
Arr. by L. G.

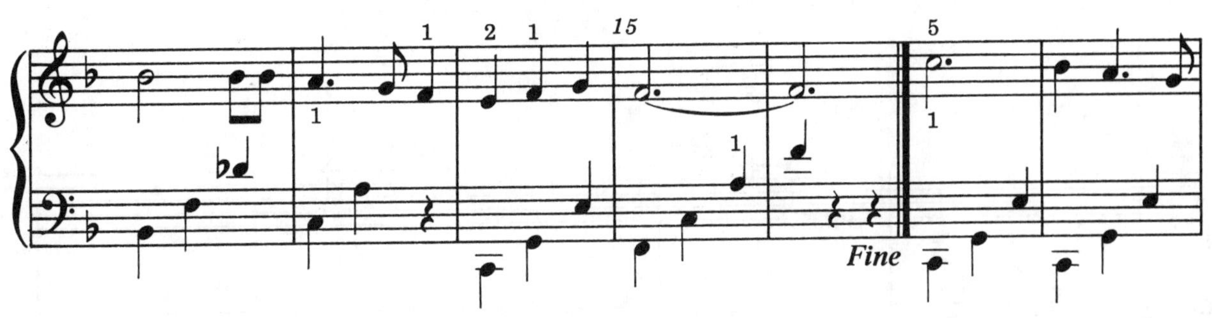

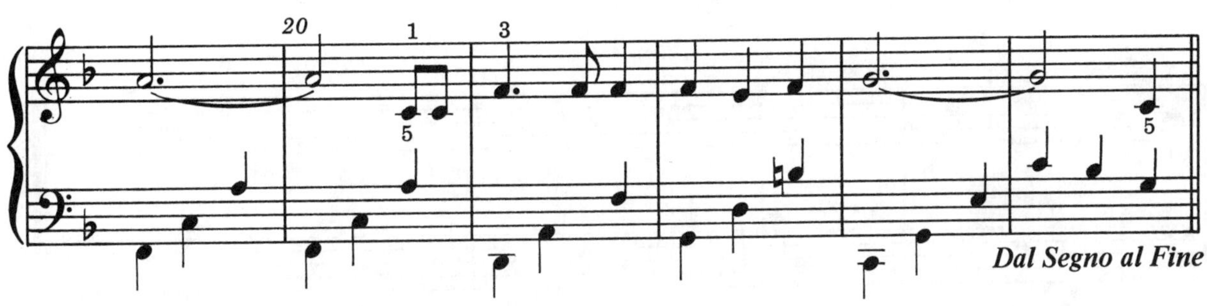

2. DIALOG

Kabalevsky

Hands Together, with Accompaniment in a Stable Hand Position

Transpose selections 1-4 to the keys listed with each selection. While playing, scan the accompaniments in quick glances while maintaining the continuity of the melody.

TWO FOLK SONGS

1. a, d, g, e

Russia

2. C, F, G, D

U. S.

3. ERIE CANAL

a, d, b, g

U. S.
Arr. by L. G.

Repeat "Erie Canal" with the following ostinato.

Repeat, doubling the speed of the ostinatos.

4. VILLAGE DANCE

C, G, D

Bartók

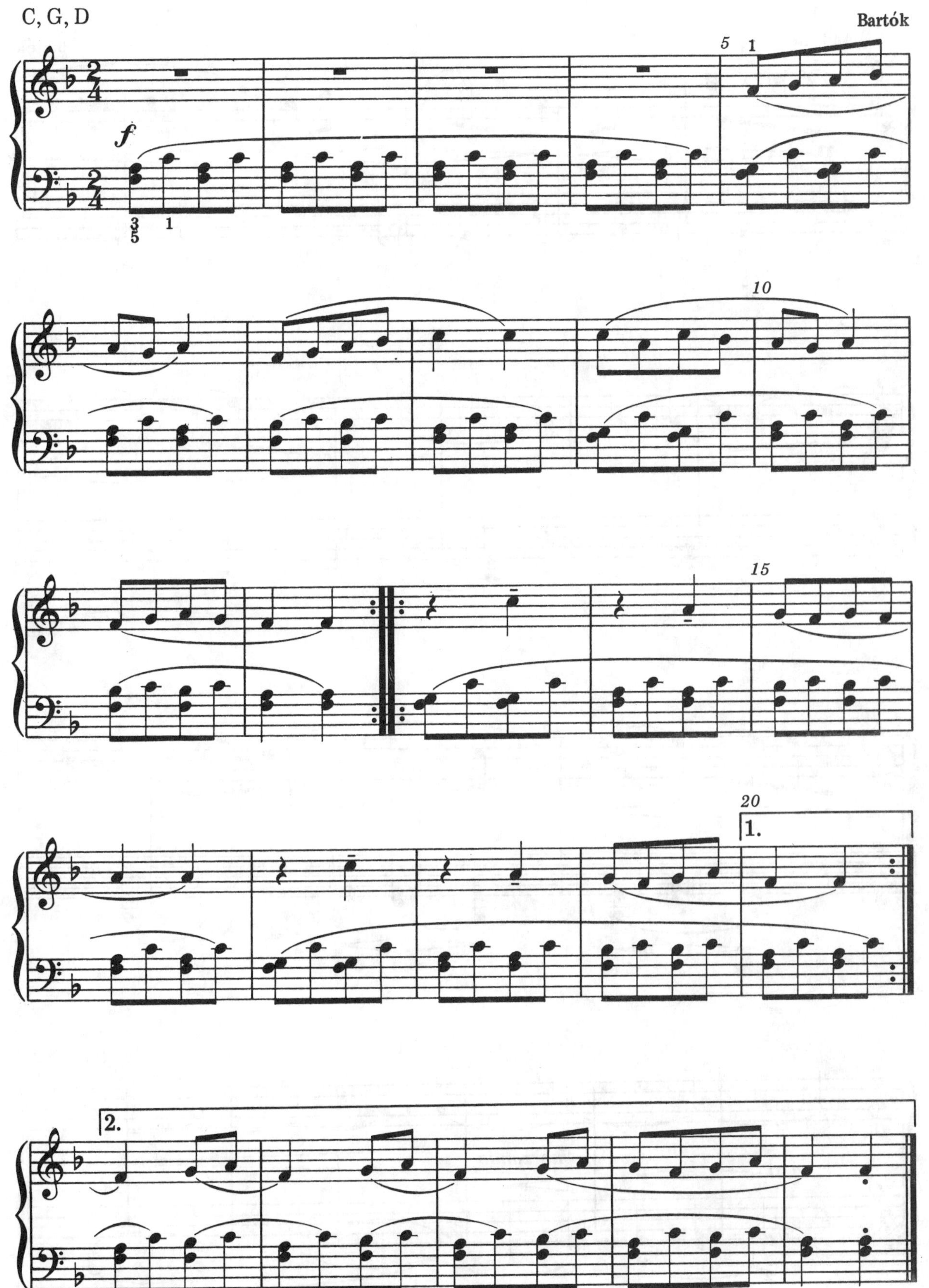

5. FROM *FOR CHILDREN*, NO. 3

6. THE ORPHAN'S SONG

7. MIXOLYDIAN SONG

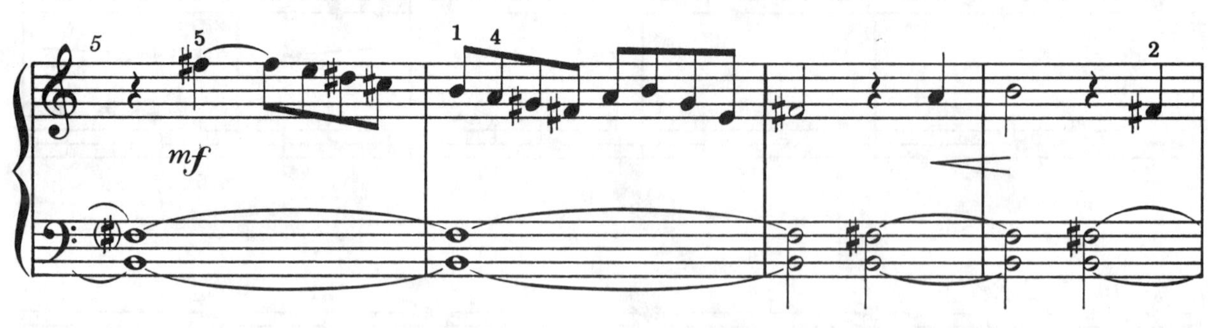

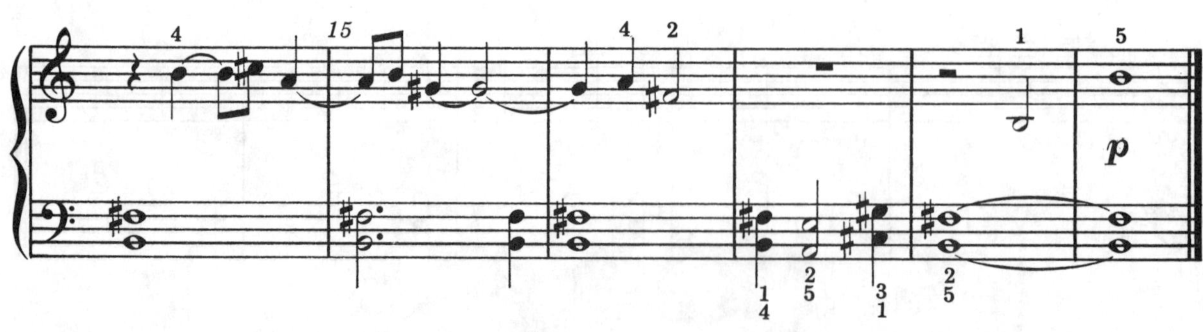

Duets: Secondos for Vertical Reading, Primos for Linear Reading

In reading notes stacked vertically on the staff, shape your hand to fit the intervals within each vertical structure. Identifying the chord by name is useful, but you should associate it as quickly as possible with its keyboard shape.

While you read, scan ahead for chord changes, being aware of which voices repeat the same pitch and the direction and distance of movement in the voices that change pitch.

For fluency in melodic reading, place your fingers on the keys as accurately as possible. When playing duets, you must count, either aloud or silently, in order to keep your place within the measure.

1. LITTLE RONDO (EXCERPT)

Josef Löw

2. ALLEGRO ALLA TURCA

8va
I
II
p
ff
p
4
8va
10
f
ff
f
1
8va
15
f
ff

TECHNIQUE

Parallel Motion for Ease with Key Signatures

Play in the key of the composition to be read.

SIGHT READING

Intervallic Reading in Contrapuntal Texture

The first two selections are in parallel motion, with identical intervals and rhythm in both hands. They may be done slowly at first, allowing time to move your hand between slurs, then playing in time. Keep time by counting aloud a specific number of beats between slurs. Repeat at successively faster tempos, reducing the number of beats to speed up hand movement between slurs.

For "Autumn Song," set a tempo consistent with the title and melodic movement of the piece.

1. AUTUMN SONG

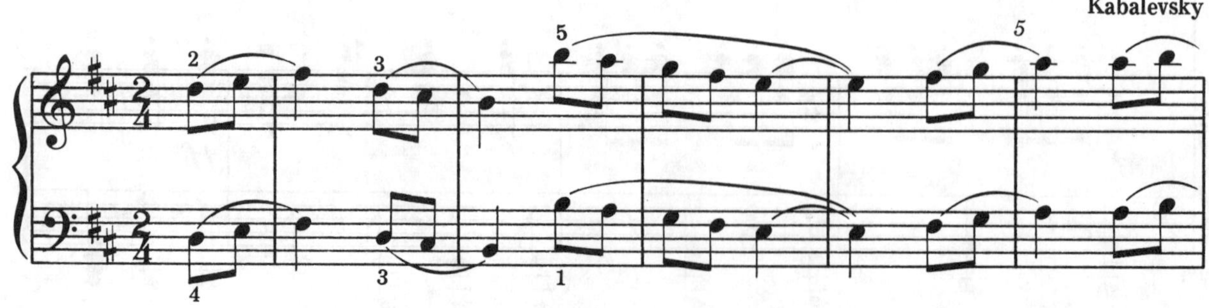

Transpose to the keys of a, e, d, and g.

2. LULLABY

Kabalevsky

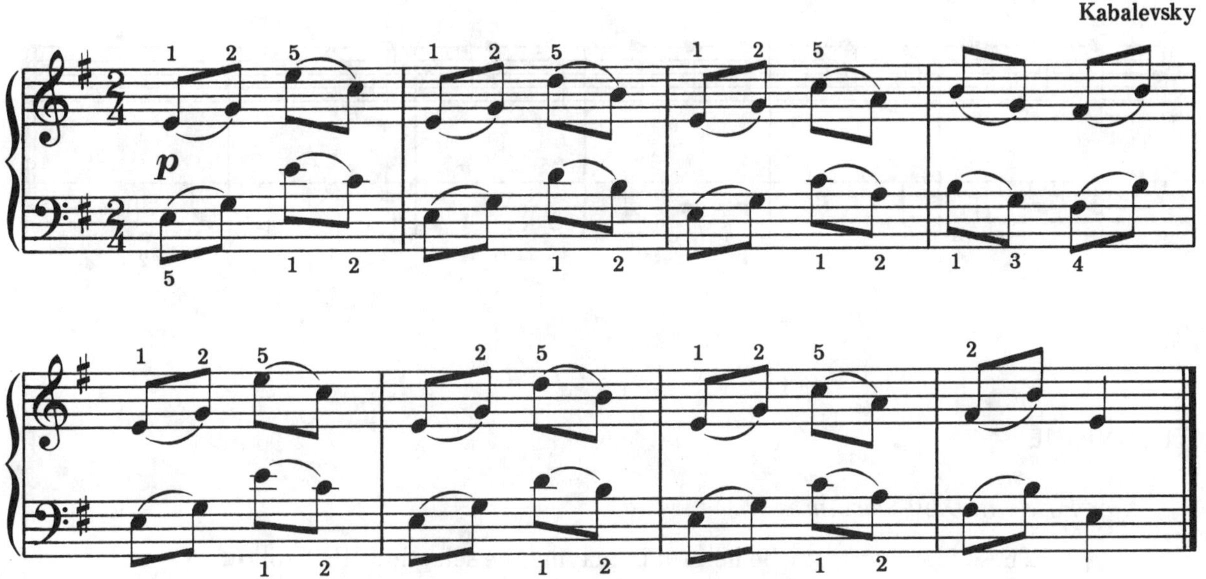

Transpose to the keys of a, b, d, and g.

The next selection gives practice in all kinds of contrapuntal motion, with intervals and rhythms varying between the hands. This selection, in the key of C, requires only that intervals be identified and played accurately and the fingering observed, with no need to recall specific sharps or flats. If you cannot maintain the beat even at a very slow tempo, read first in primary movement (see p. 105).

3. MINUET

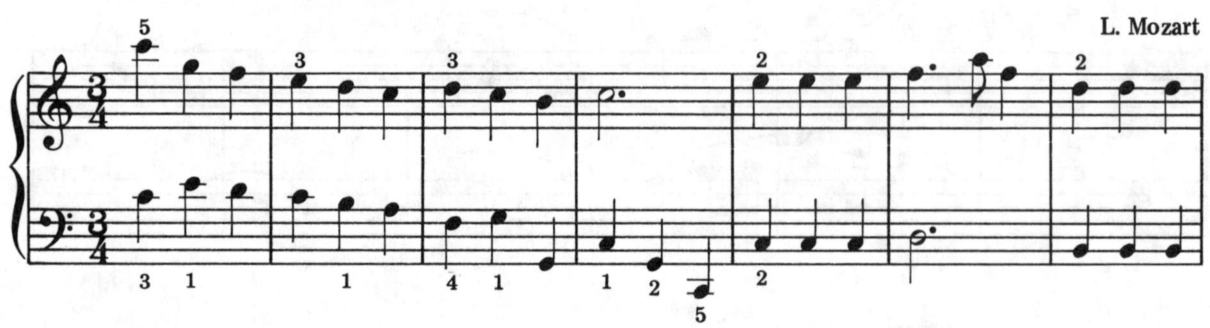

TECHNIQUE

For Ease with Key Signatures

These four steps may be helpful in playing the selections that follow.

1. Establish the keyboard track of the basic scale for the piece to be read, as suggested on page 115.

You may want to play tetrachords in clusters from each scale degree (see p. 115), fixing in your visual memory the location of the black keys in the scale.

2. Play the scale hands-together two octaves up and down, using only the index fingers, as follows.

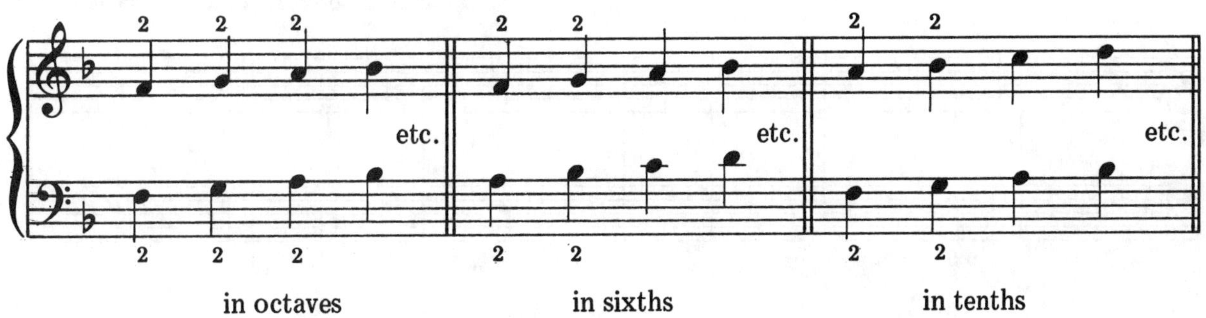

3. Play the scale in contrary motion, out and in, two octaves.

4. Play the following exercises in the key of the piece to be read.

1. CHORALE

From *Notebook for Anna Magdalene Bach*

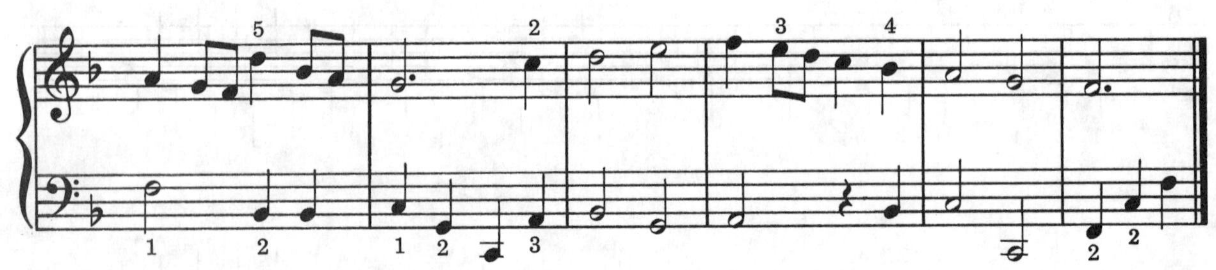

2. FOR NANNERL

L. Mozart

3. MINUET

From *Notebook for Anna Magdalene Bach*

5
20
3
1
5

1
1
2
1
3
4
2
1
1

25
5
5
5
2
3
1
2
1

1
1
30
32
1
4
5
4
2
1
2
5

4. MINUET

Four-Voiced Choral Texture

Music written in four-part harmony (that is, bass, tenor, alto, and soprano) is easiest to play if the reader keeps track of the movement in each voice. In reading the following notation, always look for voices that are stationary from one chord to the next. Scan and plan ahead. In measure 1, for example, the repetition of all four notes and the rhythm can be grasped in one swift glance. While playing that measure, plan for the voice movement on the first beat of measure 2.

To reinforce this procedure, transpose the Schytte chorale to a, d, g, and b. In each case, the raised seventh degree will be a black key.

1. CHORALE

Ludwig Schytte

2. STUDY

Victor Duvernoy

The Schumann chorale requires more complicated movement. You want to do a first reading in primary movement. Note the finger substitution for legato in measure 3 and the two different fingerings for measures 5-7 and 13-15.

3. CHORALE

REPERTOIRE

Practice Procedure

In learning the following pieces, use the suggestions given in previous units. Concentrate on hearing the rhythm and melody through vocalization, preparing hand positions, and simulating hand movement away from the keys before playing. If necessary, review pages 20, 38, and 73.

Most compositions are best prepared hands-separately first. *Caution:* Do not practice for fluency (that is, "learn") the part for each hand before playing hands-together. As early as possible, play hands-together, as slowly as necessary for maintaining the beat.

Additional suggestions for learning "A Joke," page 190:

1. Scan to identify the basic structure of the piece.
   a. Hands always on root position, white-key triads, with thumbs one step apart
   b. Pitch and rhythm pattern one measure long, repeated throughout.
   c. Basic pattern moves up and down by steps for twelve measures, then by thirds twice, to a final step to C
2. Hear the sound of pitch and rhythm mentally.
3. Place the fingers silently on the complete hand position for both hands.

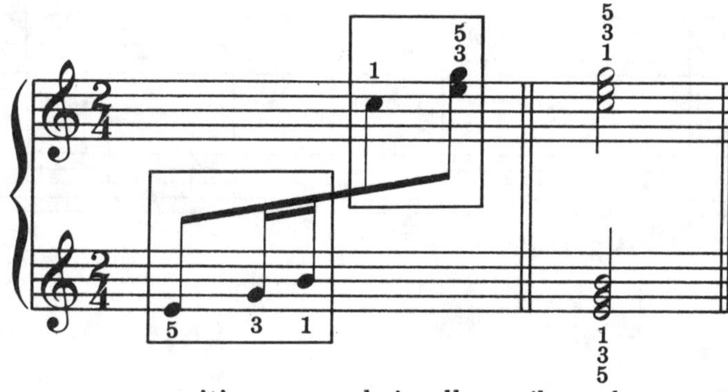

position scanned visually   silent placement

Take as much time as you need to identify the next position accurately; then move directly to it. Repeat the whole process if necessary. At this point, it is often useful to do a harmonic analysis of the score (pp. 62-63).

4. Play each position as a cluster. Count aloud "1 and 2 and" or "1, 2," while playing the clusters staccato. Move your hand to be ready to play the next cluster on the first beat of the next measure.

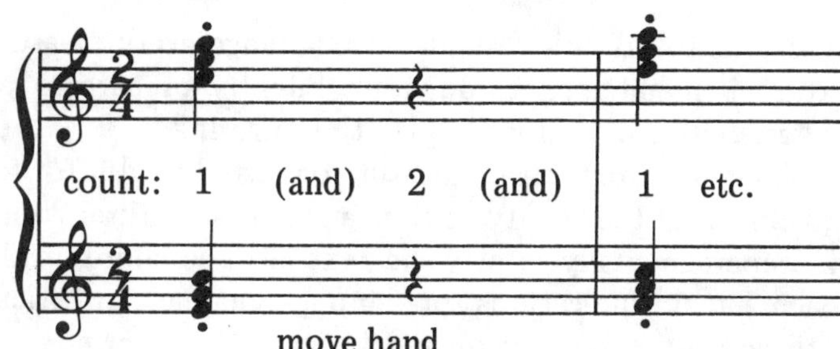

5. Before playing as written, practice the fingering and articulation of phrases in correct rhythm on the closed fallboard of the piano, moving the hands in the direction of the pitch movement.
6. Play as written, adjusting the tempo to your ability to play accurately *in time.*
7. Increase the speed to the desired tempo as fluency develops.

1. A JOKE

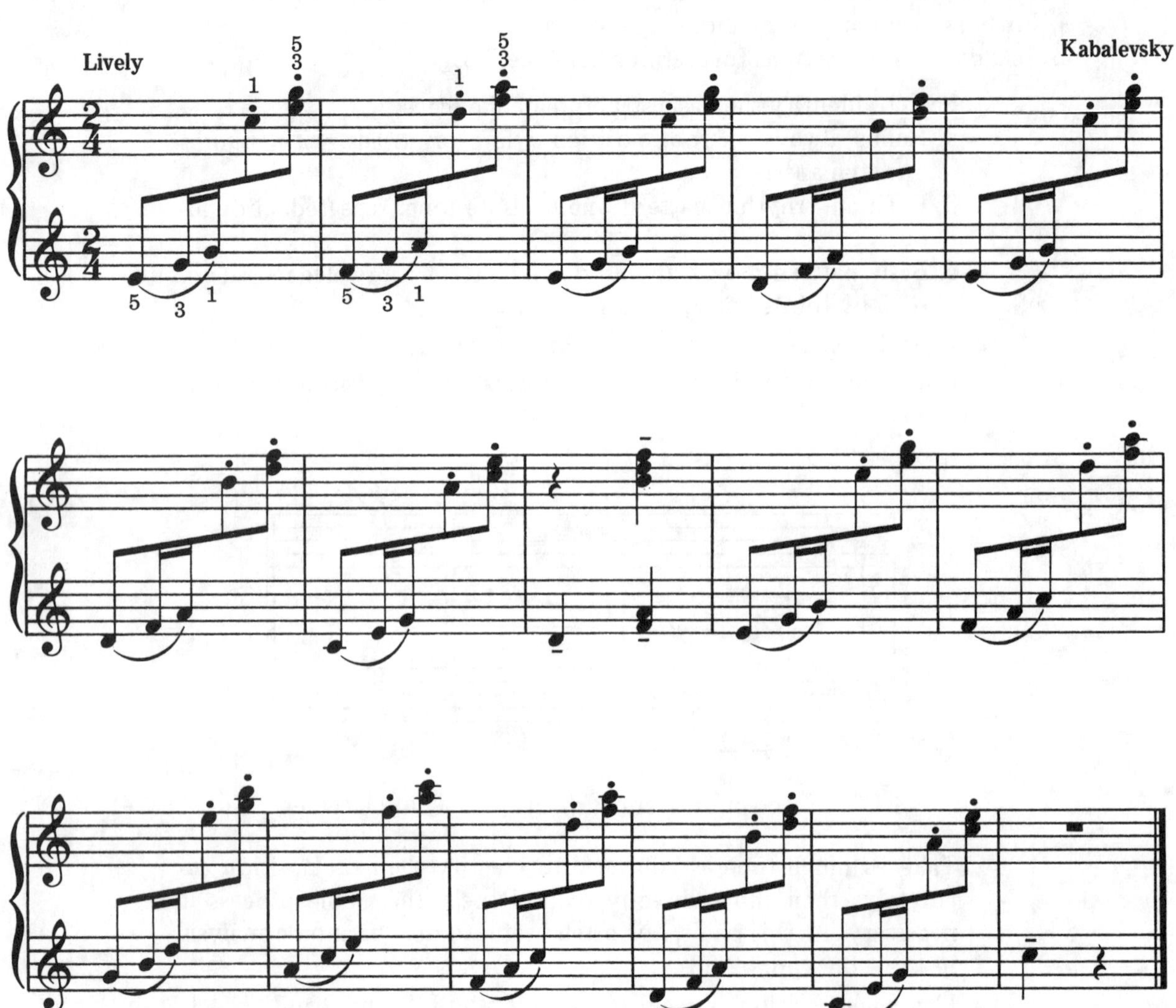

Hand positions for Bach's Prelude in C change every measure; a five-voiced texture is maintained throughout. Silently prepare to play both hands simultaneously, and carefully plan the fingering.

Play the blocked chord for each measure once and hold it for four beats; you will quickly hear the beauty of the harmonic structure. While holding one chord, prepare mentally to play the next blocked chord on time.

Since Bach left no indications for tempo, dynamics, or articulation in his scores, these matters become optional with each performer.

2. PRELUDE IN C MAJOR
(From *The Well-Tempered Clavier*, Book I)

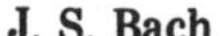
J. S. Bach

15
20

25
30
35

3. MUSETTE

From *Notebook for Anna Magdalene Bach*

4. THE BEAR

Heavily

Shostakovitch

25

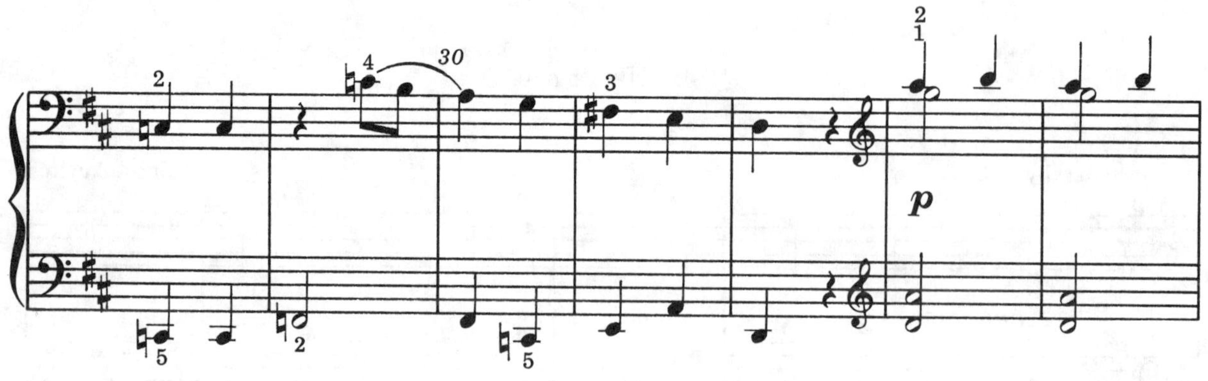
30
p

35
40
f
p

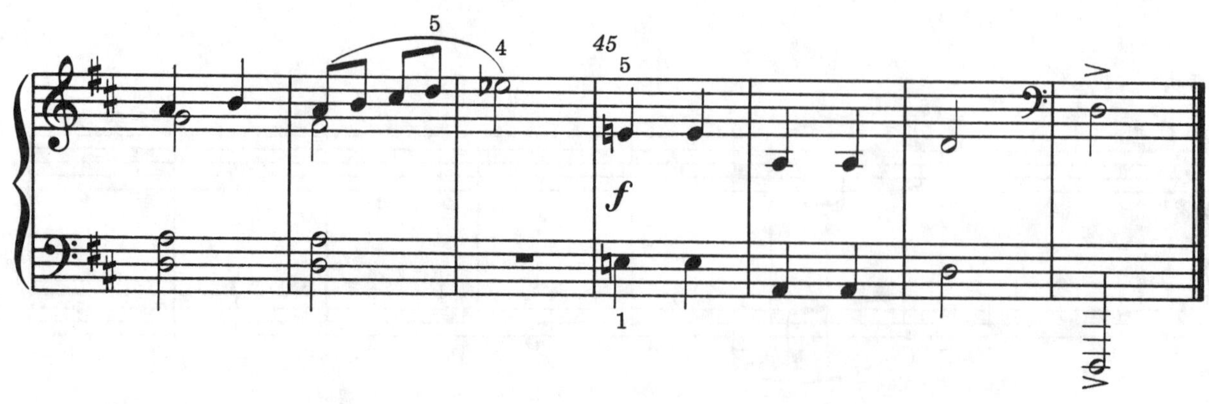
45
f

5. DANCE

Kabalevsky

6. NOSTALGIA

20
rit.
a tempo
pp
25
f
pp
30
p
35
rit.
a tempo
pp

7. FROM *For Children*, No. 26

© Copyright 1946 by Boosey & Hawkes, Inc. Renewed 1973. Reprinted by permission.

8. ROUND DANCE

Béla Bartók

© Copyright 1946 by Boosey & Hawkes, Inc. Renewed 1973. Reprinted by permission.

9. ARMES WAISENKIND (The Poor Little Orphan)

20
Langsamer

In Tempo
25

30

10. OLD FRENCH SONG (From *Album for the Young*)

11. FUGUE

Primo: right hand *8va* higher throughout.

Handel
Arr. by L. G.

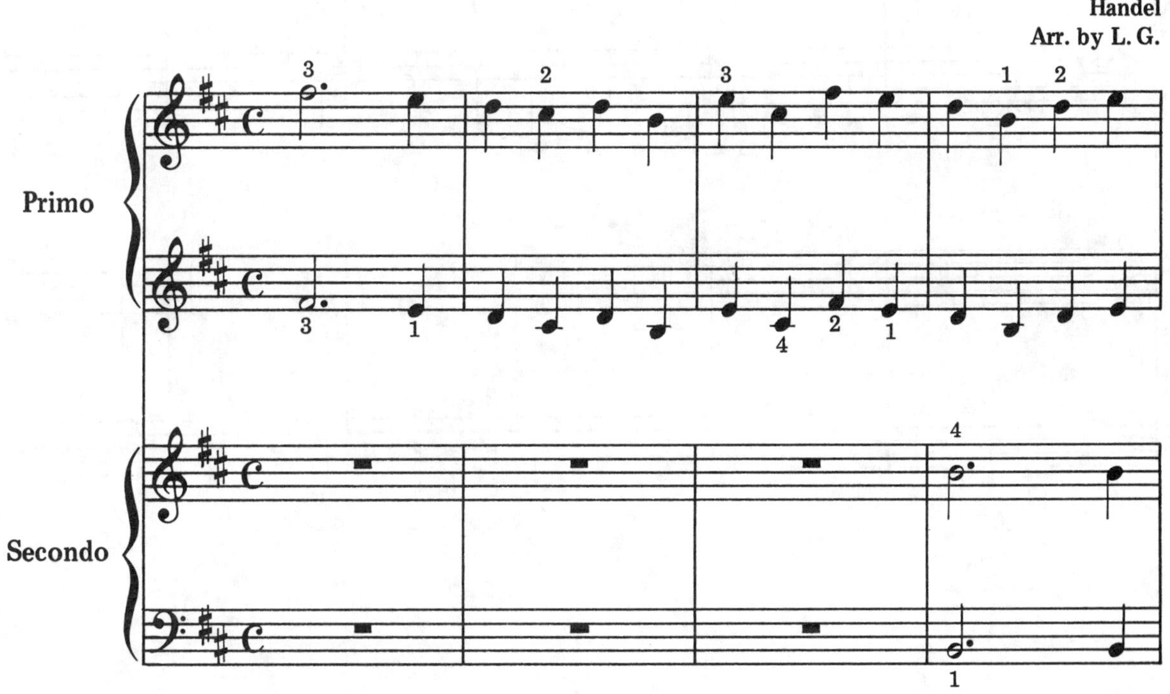

I
II
15
8va

I
II
20
continue 8va throughout

25
I
II

30
I
II
8va

12. FESTIVAL

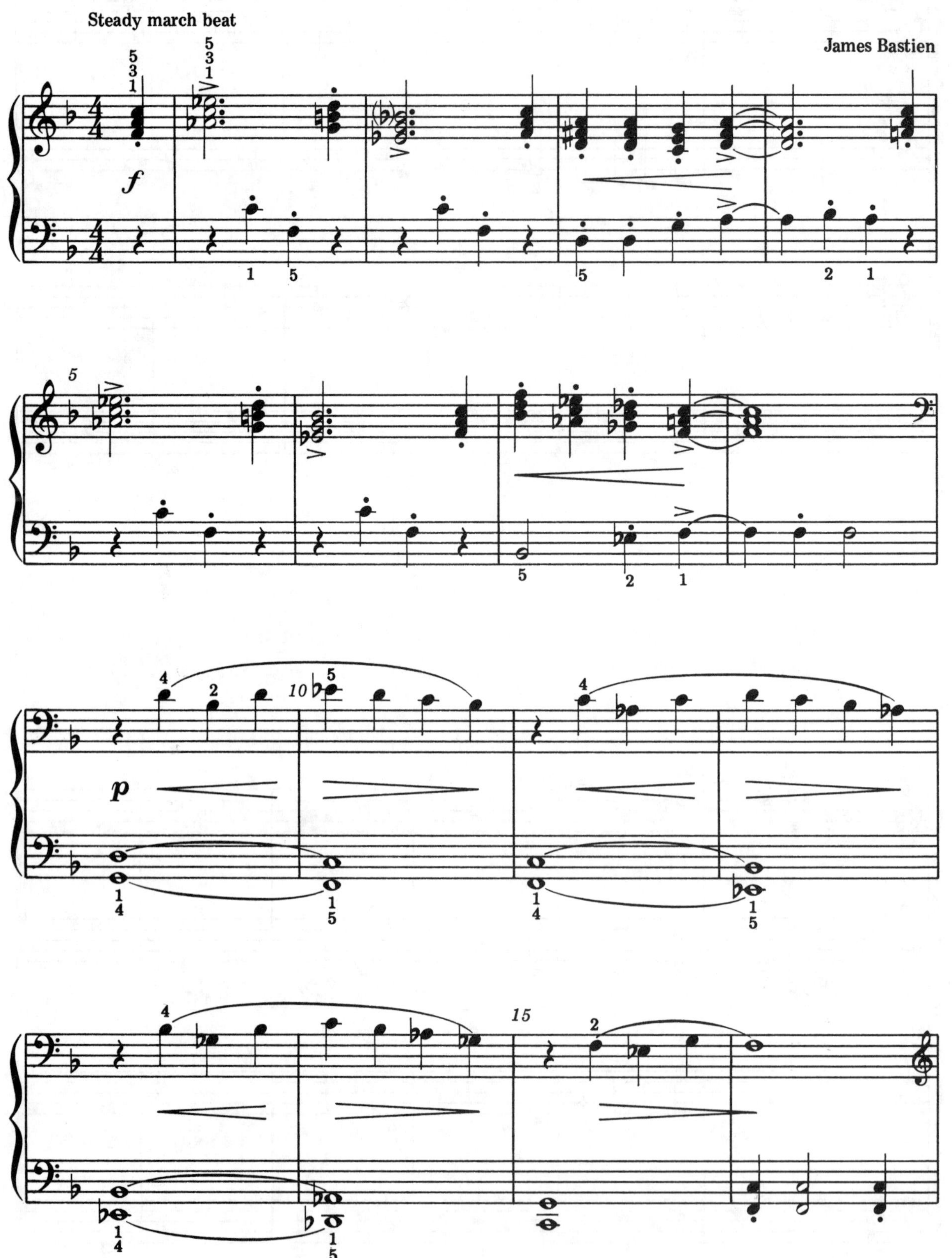

Used by permission. © 1973 General Words and Music Company, Park Ridge, Ill.

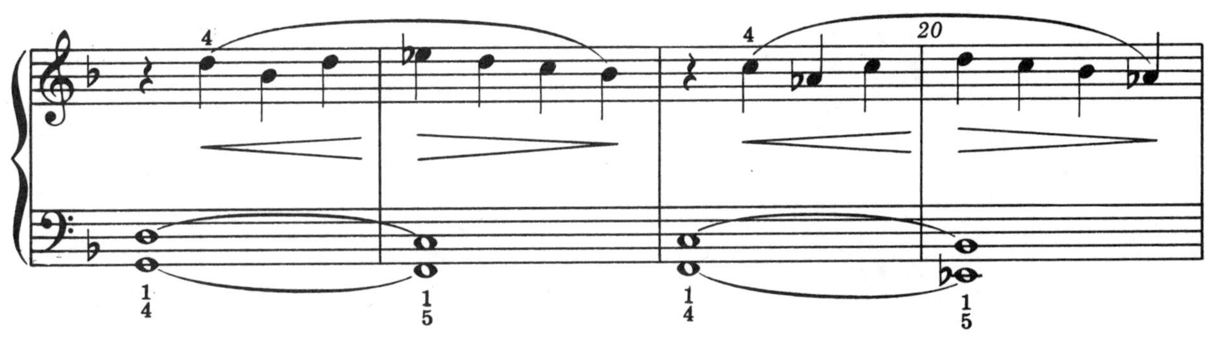

20

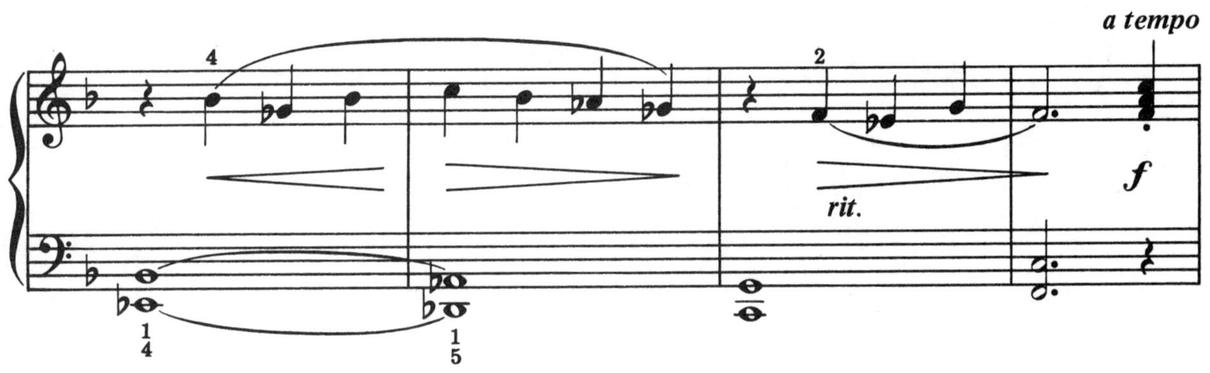

a tempo
rit.
f

25

30
rit.
8va

UNIT EIGHT

Completing the Cycle of Keys

Unit 8 presents the remaining key signatures in the cycle: those containing from three to seven sharps or flats.

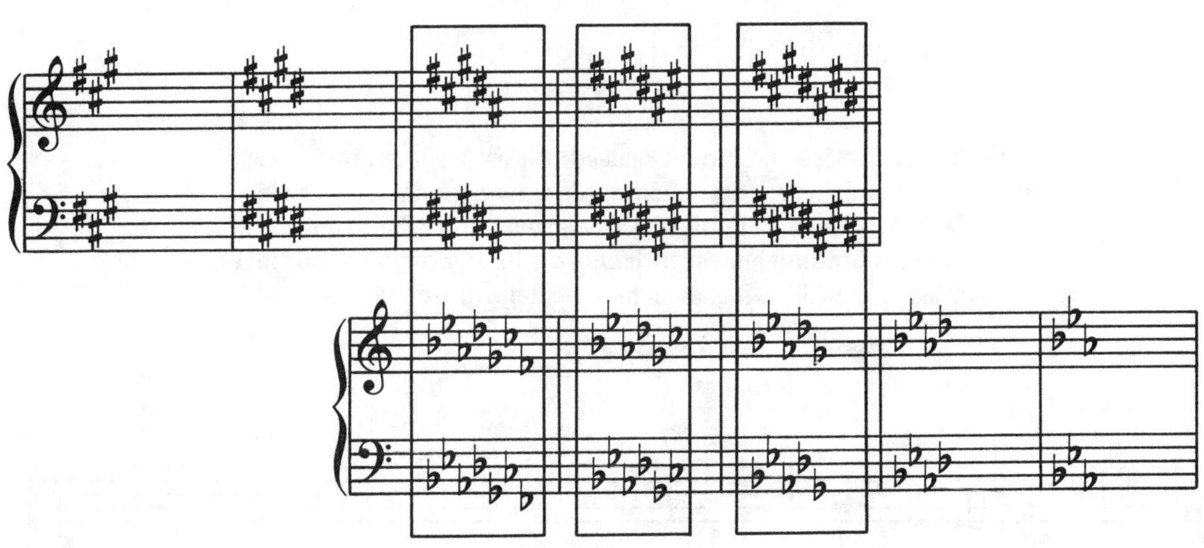

enharmonic equivalents

Of these signatures, those whose scales include all the black piano keys—B (C♭), F♯ (G♭), and D♭ (C♯)—include only two white keys each. Thus you can recall their keyboard tracks more easily than the tracks for the signatures of three and four sharps and flats; when playing them, you need to remember only which two white keys to play.

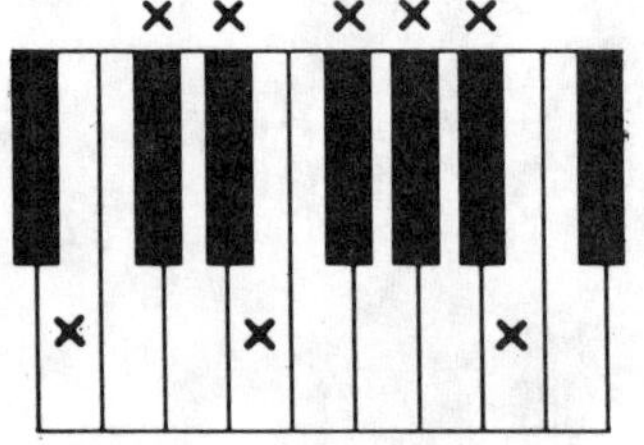

B(C♭), lower of each two white keys

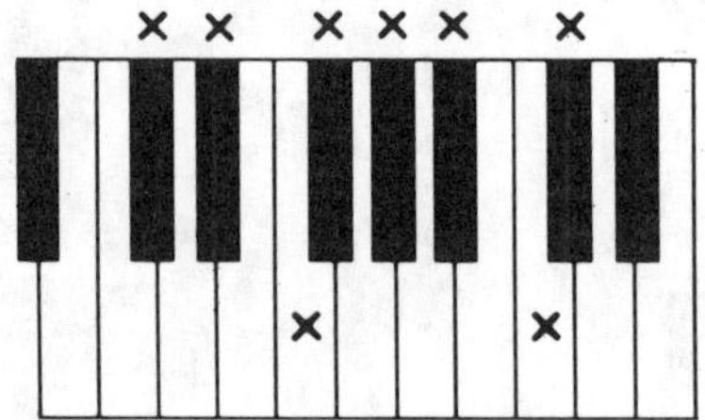

D♭ (C♯), upper white key

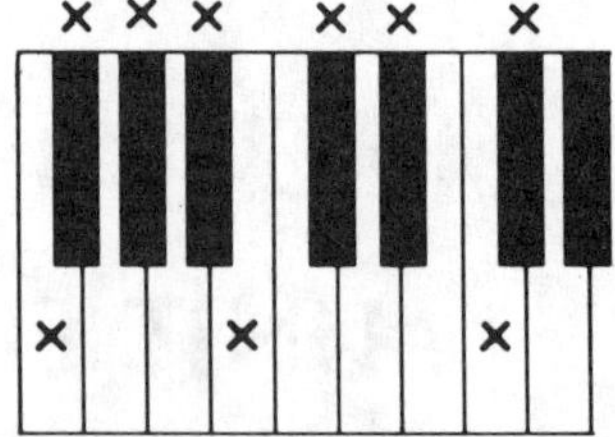

F♯ (G♭), white keys bracket the three-black-key group

TECHNIQUE

Playing Scales Hands-Together: B, F♯, D♭

The three scale systems in which all the black keys occur are the easiest for the pianist to play hands-together because the fingering is easy to control. (The term *system* refers to all seven modal scales to which a key signature may apply.) The thumbs play white keys and the long fingers play the black keys: on the group of two black keys, R.H. 2-3, L.H. 3-2; on the three black keys, R.H. 2-3-4, L.H. 4-3-2.

Keys of B(C♭), F♯(G♭), D♭(C♯)

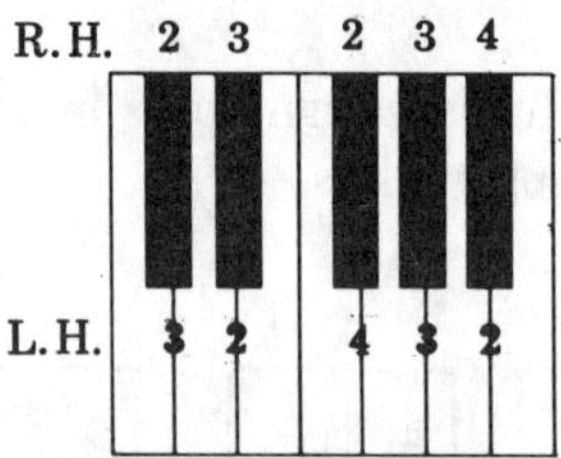

It is useful to practice the modal scales both as preparation for jazz improvisation and to gain security in a key. (Jazz uses modal labels to indicate which scale may be used to improvise to a given chord; for example, Mixolydian scale with a dominant seventh chord.) In working out the fingering for a given scale, the following steps may be helpful.

1. Block the scale (B major)

2. Practice the scale in rhythms. Play the scale two octaves up and down in ♩ and in ♫, three octaves up and down in ♩♩♩ (triplet).
3. Fingering for B major and related modes. The outlines indicate that the thumbs play together.

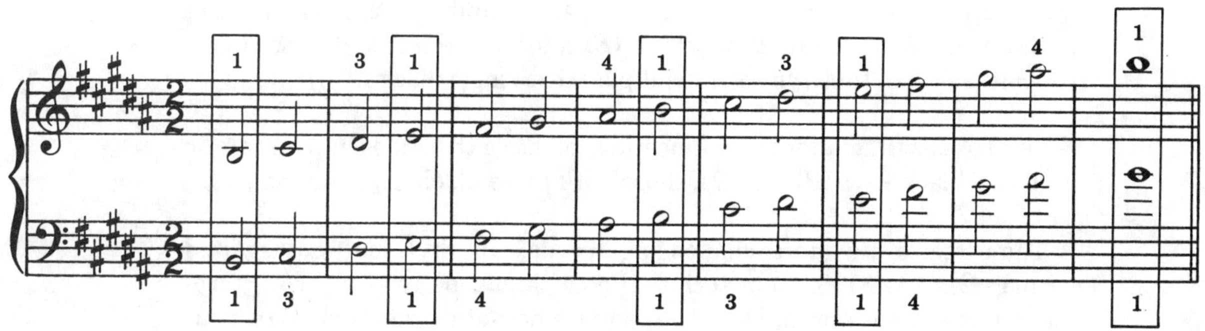

Dorian

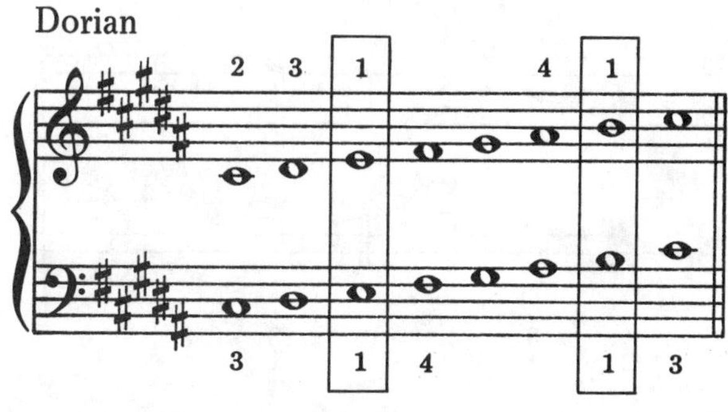

Phrygian

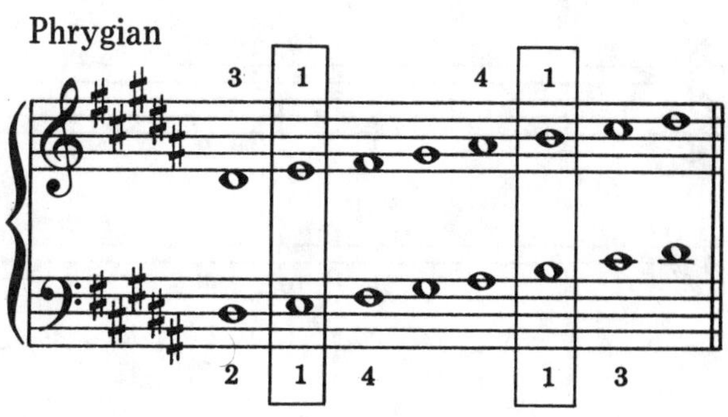

Lydian

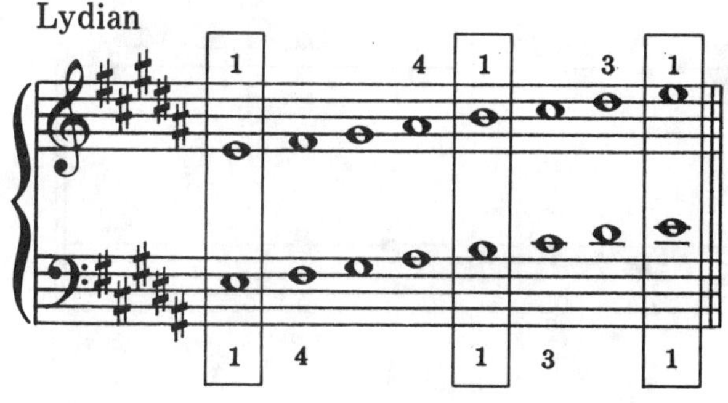

Mixolydian

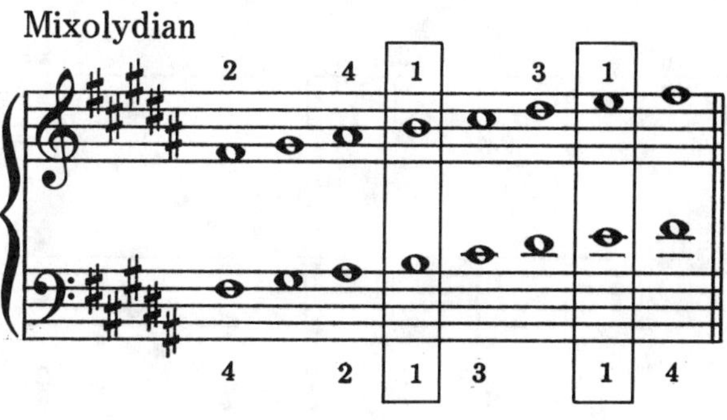

Aeolian

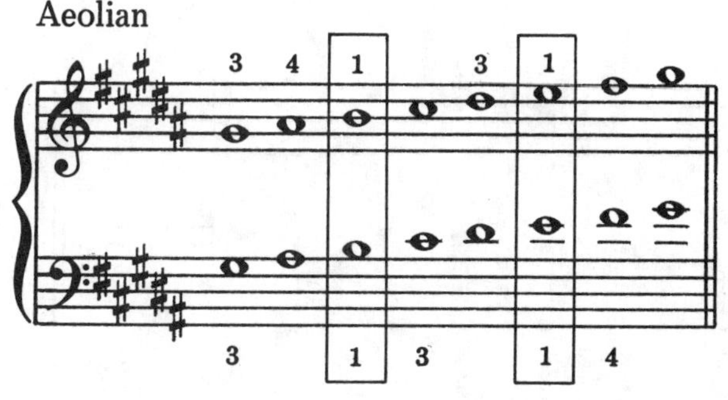

Locrian

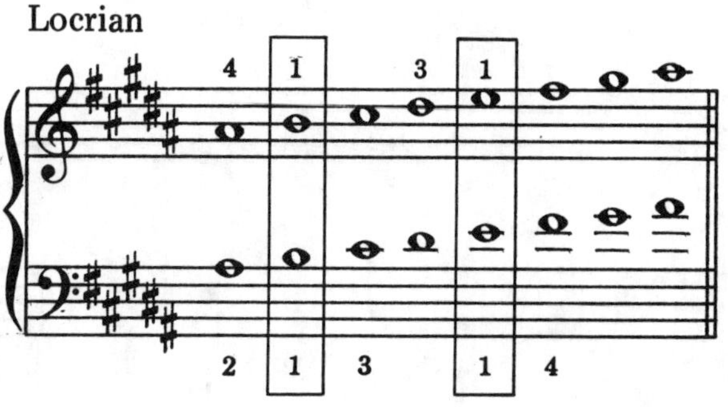

Playing Scales Hands-Together: All Other Keys

For all the scales in which fewer than five black keys occur, more than one comfortable fingering is possible. The most widely accepted traditional fingering is shown closest to the notes in the following scores. In the alternative fingering, given in parentheses, finger crossing over thumb always occurs from a white key to a black, and thumb crossing under finger occurs from a black key to a white. (*Exceptions:* the F and G scales, in which the fourth finger in each hand plays the single black key.)

Note: To learn the alternative fingering, practice the scales in pairs: those with two black keys (B♭ and D), those with three black keys, and so on.

These scales are more challenging to play in rhythms, as suggested on page 213. The minimum technical goal should be to play two octaves up and down, with even, clear tone and no hesitation, at a tempo of your choice.

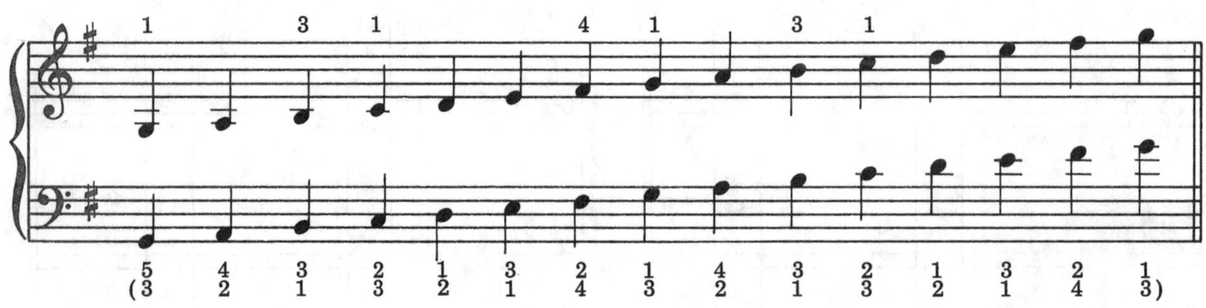

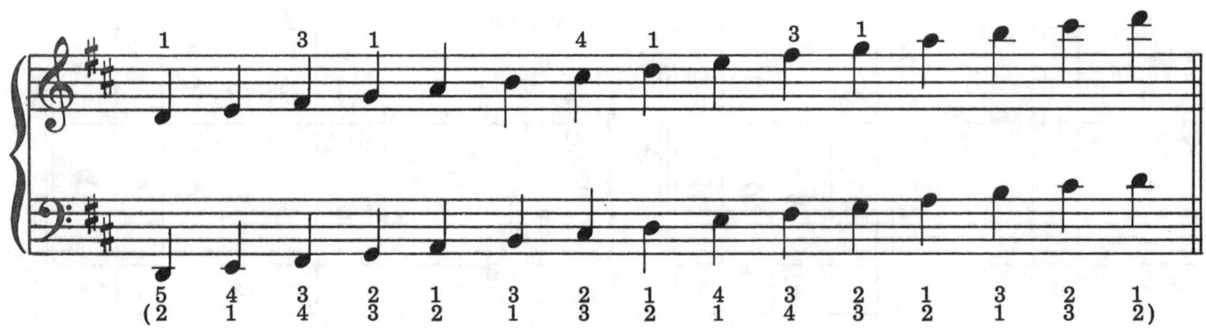

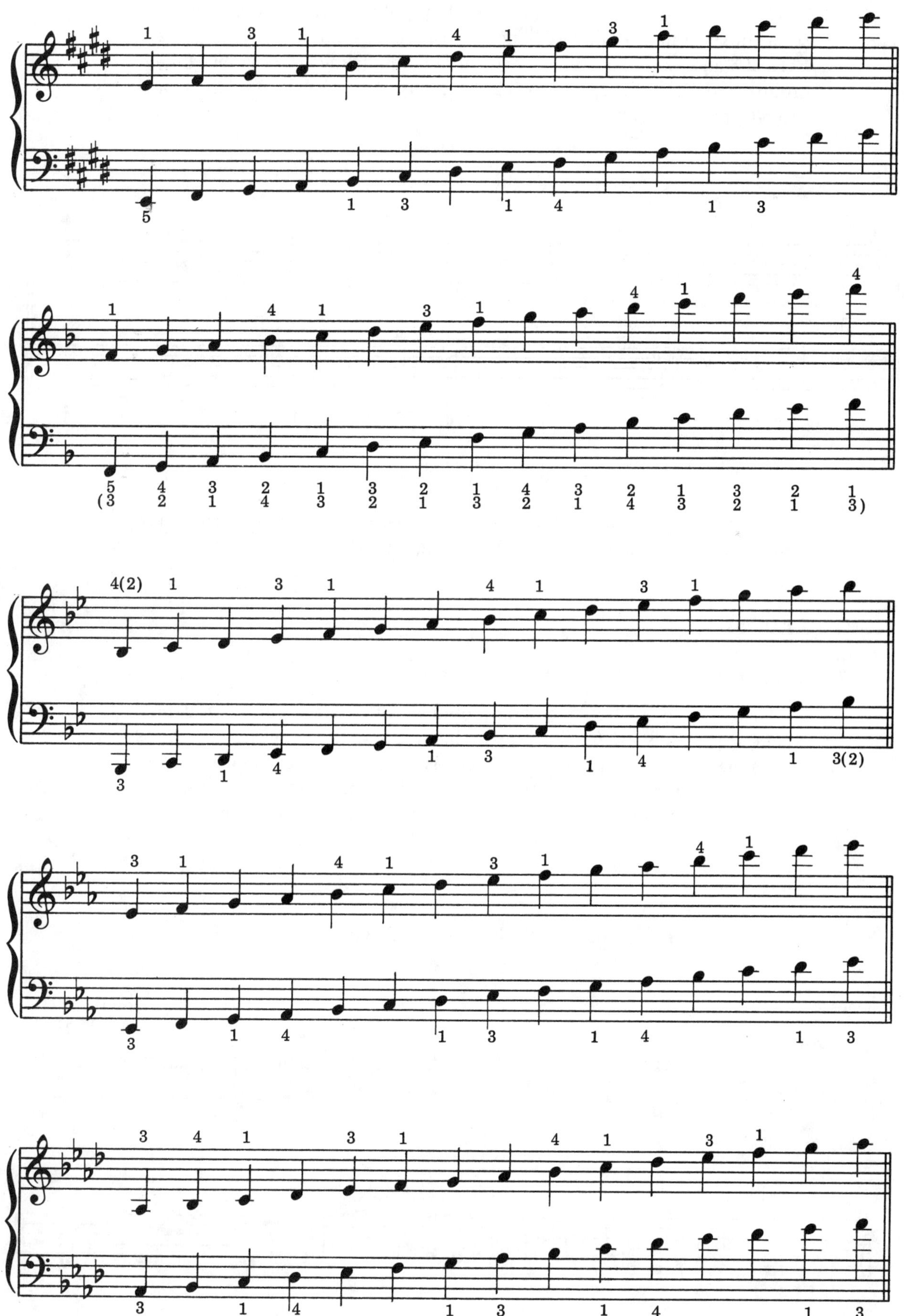
1
3
1
4
1
3
1
5
1
3
1
4
1
3
1
4
1
3
1
4
1
4
5
4
3
2
1
3
2
1
4
3
2
1
3
2
1
(3
2
1
4
3
2
1
3
2
4
3
2
1
3)
4(2)
1
3
1
4
1
3
1
3
1
4
1
3
1
4
1
3(2)
3
1
4
1
3
1
4
1
3
1
4
1
3
1
4
1
3
3
4
1
3
1
4
1
3
1
3
1
4
1
3
1
4
1
3

The remaining scale, with no black keys, also offers fingering alternatives. In the one for the left hand given here, the thumbs play together; R.H. 2-3 and L.H. 3-2 are grouped on D-E (guideline: the two-black-key group); and R.H. 2-3-4, L.H. 4-3-2 are grouped on G-A-B (guideline: the three-black-key group).

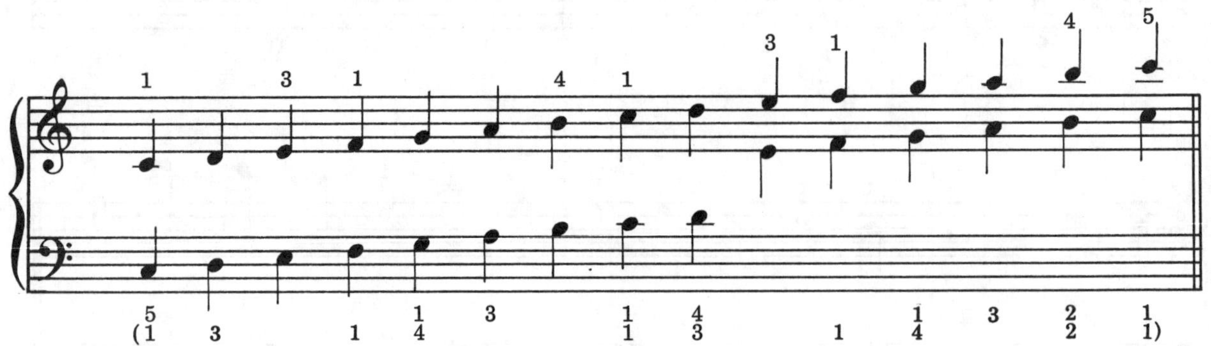

You may prefer the fingering given on page 117, although that may prove to be more difficult to play hands-together than the one given above.

SIGHT READING

Transposing as an Aid to Recall of Key Signature

These melodies should be transposed to other keys *before* you play them in the key of C. Singing, or hearing mentally, before playing is recommended. Although a specific key is suggested for each melody, you may prefer to transpose all into the same key, in order to develop security with that key; transposition into the various keys may be done at a later time.

1. THEME FROM BAGATELLE OP. 119, NO. 3

Suggested key: A

2. SWISS FOLK TUNE

Suggested key: E♭

3. LUSTIG

Suggested key: E

Beethoven

4. LA ROXELANE

Suggested key: g

Haydn

5. MY SWEET REPOSE

Suggested key: A♭

Schubert

6. THE GUIDEPOST

Suggested key: f

Schubert

7. ALLEGRETTO FROM SYMPHONY NO. 85

Suggested key: E♭

Haydn

8. SPRING DREAMS

Applying Two Key Signatures to a Given Score

As you saw earlier (p. 114), the same pitch notation may be used for two "alternate keys"; that is, a melody or complete composition notated in D major, for example, may also be read in the key of D♭. Each of the following melodies and compositions should be played in both keys listed.

Selections 1-4: keys of D and D♭ (or b and b♭).

1. LI'L LIZA JANE

2. JOHNNY HAS GONE FOR A SOLDIER

3. O GOD, BENEATH WHOSE GUIDING HAND

John Hatton

4. KING WILLIAM'S MARCH

Jeremiah Clarke

Note: Fingering may be changed for the key of D♭.

Selections 5-9: keys of B and B♭ (or g♯ and g)

5. BEN BOLT

U. S.

6. SILENT NIGHT

Franz Gruber

7. BLUE BELLS OF SCOTLAND

8. SHOO FLY

U. S.
Arr. by L. G.

9. COVENTRY CAROL

England
Arr. by L. G.

Selections 10-13: keys of F and F♯ (or d and d♯); G and G♭ (or e and e♭)

10. DONA NOBIS PACEM

To be played twice, ensemble, as a round

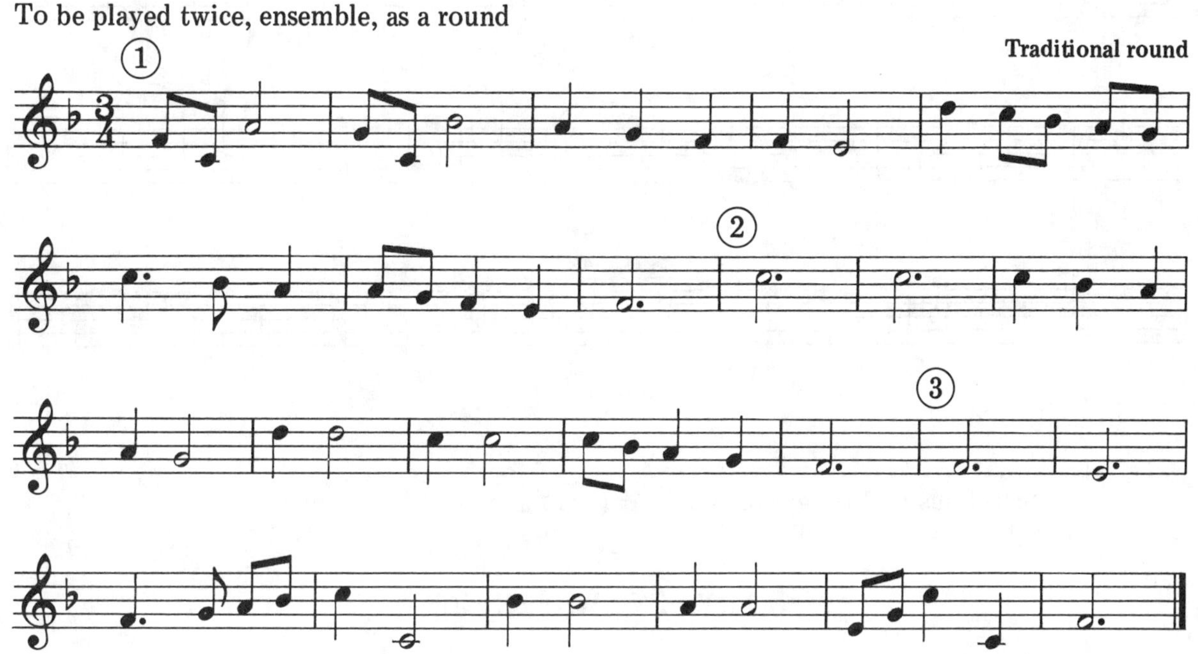

11. BRING A TORCH, JEANNETTE ISABELLA

12. ROUND

To be played twice, ensemble, as a round

13. THE SHANTY AND THE PINE

Lumberjack song

Selections 14-17: keys of A and A♭ (or f♯ and f)

14. WHEN I WAS SINGLE

U. S.

15. GOLDEN SLIPPERS

James A. Bland

16. AIR FROM *The Marriage of Figaro*

W. A. Mozart

17. ALL CREATURES OF OUR GOD AND KING

Germany

Selections 18-24: keys of E and E♭ (or c♯ and c)

18. THE FOGGY FOGGY DEW

U. S.

19. ON MY JOURNEY HOME

Spiritual

20. A FROG WENT A-COURTING

England

21. THE STREETS OF LAREDO

U. S.

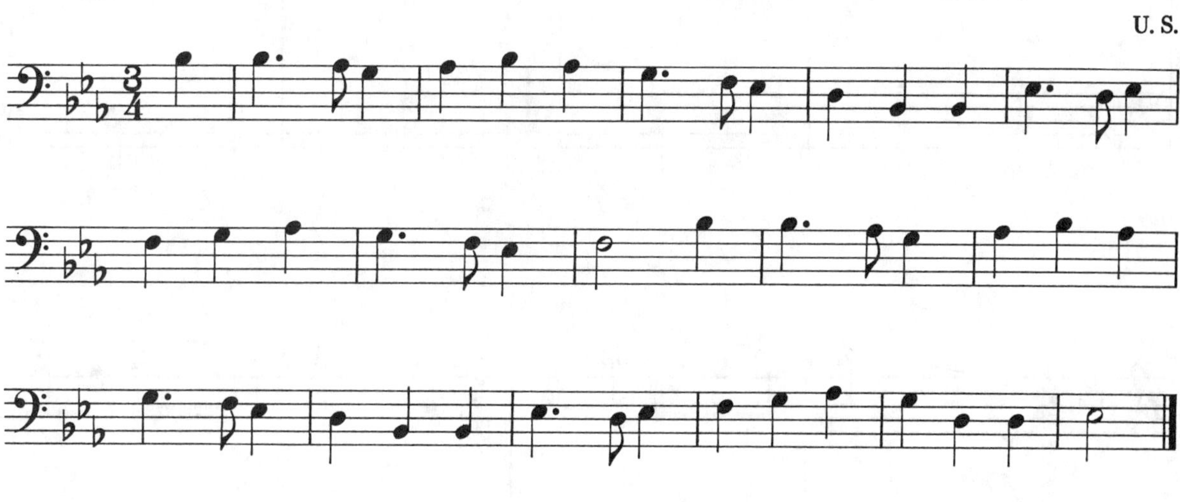

22. OLD JOE CLARK

U. S.

23. GYPSY DANCE

Allegro

Haydn

24. GERMAN DANCE

Haydn

Applying Two Key Signatures to Melody and Accompaniment

Each of the following melodies should be played and harmonized in the two alternate keys to which the notation applies. No chord symbols are given. (Selections 1-5 require only I and V.)

1. GO TELL AUNT RHODY

U. S.

2. MY HAT

Germany

3. BOW BELINDA

U. S.

4. OH WHERE, OH WHERE HAS MY LITTLE DOG GONE?

Germany

5. HUSH, LITTLE BABY

U. S.

Selections 6-13 require I, IV, and V.

6. OLD CHISHOLM TRAIL

Cowboy song

7. GOODBYE, MY LOVER, GOODBYE

Chantey

8. CIELITO LINDO

Mexico

9. GET ON BOARD

Spiritual

10. CAMPTOWN RACES

11. ALOHA OE

12. COME AND DANCE WITH ME

13. LITTLE WHEEL A-TURNING

IMPROVISATION

Playing in Seven Modes on a Constant Tonal Center

Structure F♯ as tonal center
Accompaniment: ostinato in eighth notes
Melodic phrases in modes from the "brightest," Lydian, to the "darkest," Locrian

Fingering suggestion: avoid playing the thumb on black keys. (For a summary of key signatures applied to modes, review p. 159.)

Ionian (major) mode: drop B♯ | Mixolydian mode: drop E♯

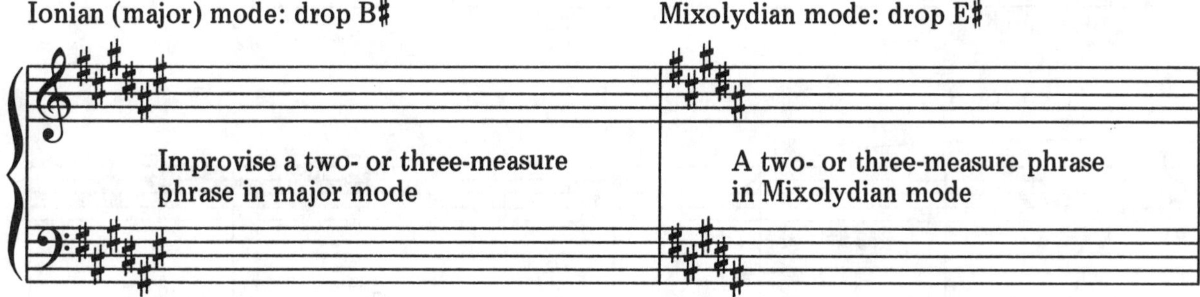

Dorian mode: drop A♯ | Aeolian (minor) mode: drop D♯

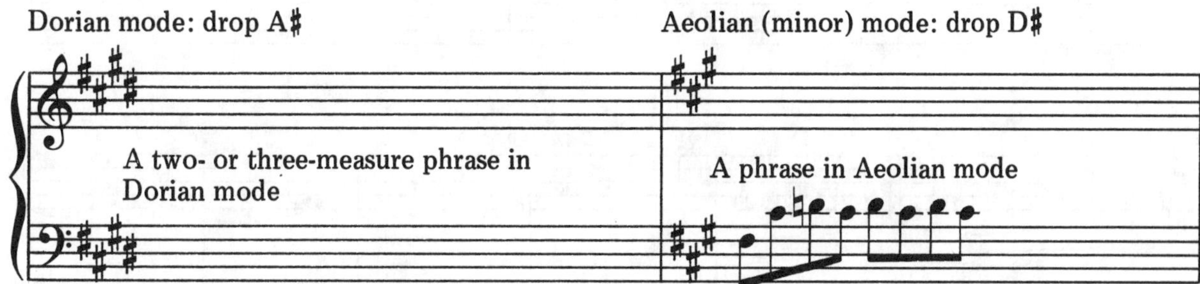

Phrygian mode: drop G♯ | Locrian mode: drop C♯

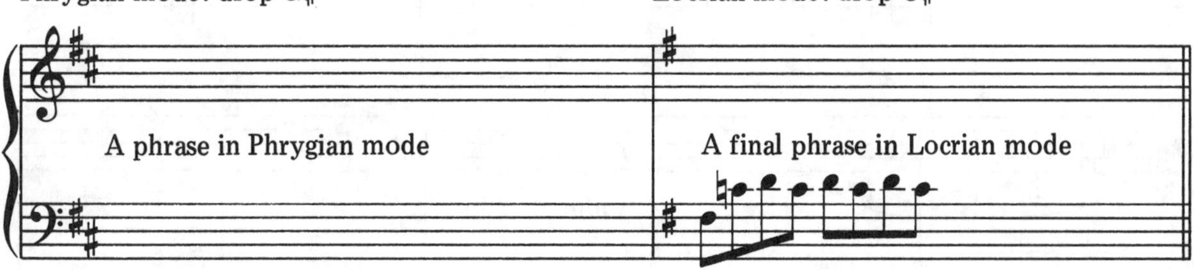

READING

Hearing Before Playing

Bartók notated "Peasant Song" without a key signature, placing the sharps in the score as accidentals.

Figure out the key signature from the score. Identify the tonal center and mode. Sing the scale on which the piece is based.

Before playing, read the score silently, hearing the melody mentally. While playing, observe the fingering accurately. As a reinforcement of intervallic reading, transpose to the key that has no sharps or flats.

PEASANT SONG

IMPROVISATION

Continuing an Incomplete Composition

Structure Free form and texture
or
Melody based on a mode of your choice (review p. 235)
Accompaniment: ostinato on page 235, or an original one

LINGERING MEMORY

L. G.

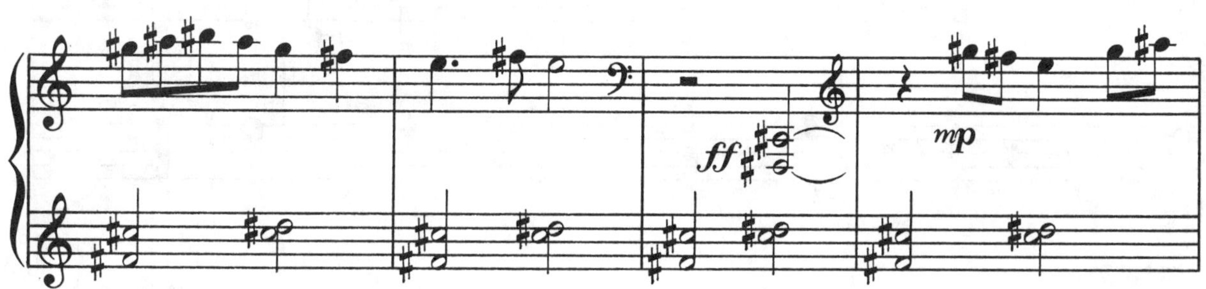

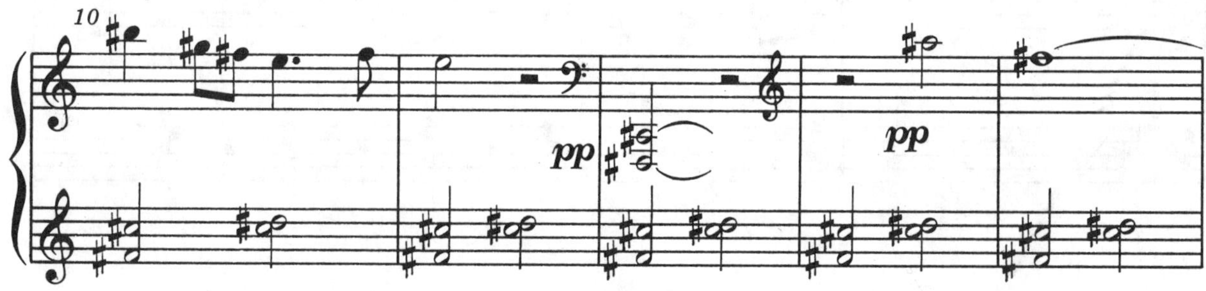

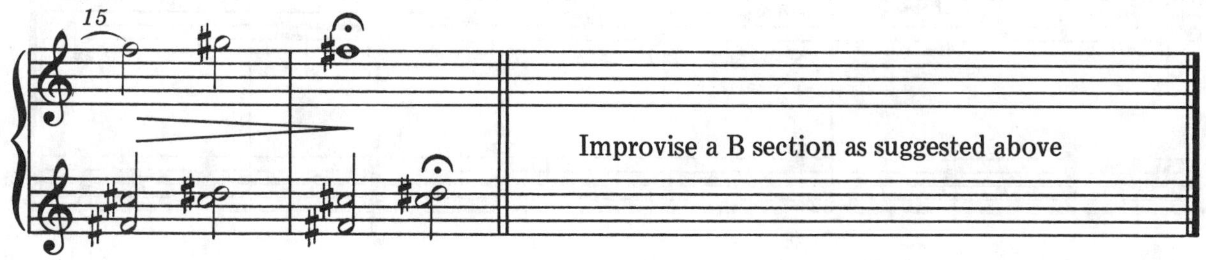

HARMONIZATION

Additonal Practice with ii⁶ in Major

Play the following selection in the keys of D and D♭.

Playing by Ear and Harmonizing from a Given Chord Outline

Play the melody of "America" by ear in the keys of G and G♭. Then play the melody and an accompaniment based on the chords given below. All chords are to be played on the beat. The Roman numerals may be used as a guide to accompaniment in G♭.

AMERICA

Words by Samuel Francis Smith **Music by Henry Carey**

G Em Am/C	D^7	G Em Am/C	G/D D♯dim^7 Em
My coun - try,	'tis of thee,	Sweet land of	lib - er - ty,
I vi ii^6	V^7	I vi ii^6	I e-vii$^o_7$ G/vi

Am/C G/D D^7	G	G	G	D/F♯
Of thee I	sing;	Land where my	fa - thers died,	Land of the
ii^6 I$^6_4$ V^7	I	I	I	V^6

D/F♯	G	G F♯dim/A G/B	C G/D D^7	G
Pil-grims' pride,	From ev - 'ry	moun - tain-side	Let free - dom	ring!
V^6	I	I vii$^o_6$ I^6	IV I$^6_4$ V^7	I

TECHNIQUE

Chords Used in Harmonizing "America"

HARMONIZATION

Melodies with ii^6

Harmonize the following melodies. In the first two, *X* marks the location of ii^6. Note that the melody note in 1 is the second degree of the scale.

1. WHEN I WAS SINGLE

U. S.

2. BARBARA ALLEN

Scotland

The location of ii^6 is not indicated in the following selections. Look and listen for the second, fourth, or sixth degrees in the melodies. Play and harmonize the pieces also in alternate keys.

3. GOLDEN SLIPPERS

James A. Bland

4. WAIT FOR THE WAGON

5. MARY AND MARTHA

Spiritual

6. HAPPY BIRTHDAY

Mildred and Patty Hill

Copyright © 1935 by Summy-Birchard Company, Evanston, Illinois. Copyright renewed 1962. All rights reserved. Used by permission.

1. THE JAM ON GERRY'S ROCKS

American logging song
Adapted by L. G.

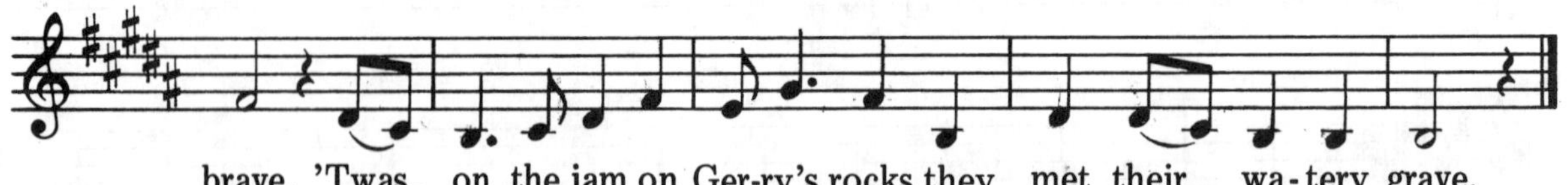

Lois Choksy, *The Kodaly Method: Comprehensive Music Education from Infant to Adult,* © 1974, No. 151. Adapted by L. G. by permission of Prentice-Hall, Inc., Englewood Cliffs, New Jersey.

2. RUSSIAN FOLK TUNE

3. OLD JOE CLARK

1. FROM *FOR CHILDREN*, NO. 2

2. FROM *FOR CHILDREN*, NO. 9

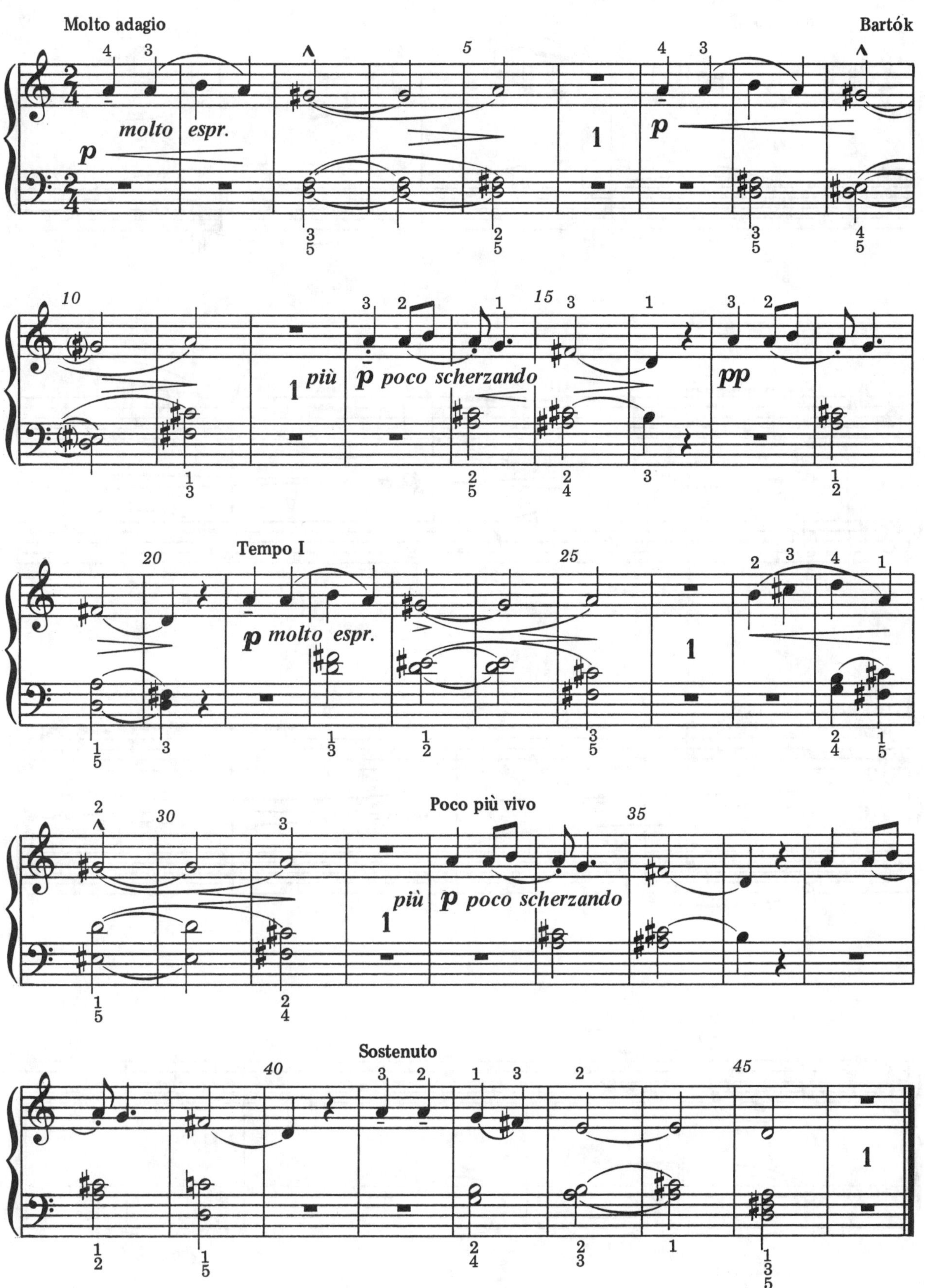

3. NIGHT ON THE RIVER

4. GERMAN DANCE

5. LITTLE SONG

6. ECOSSAISE

Schubert

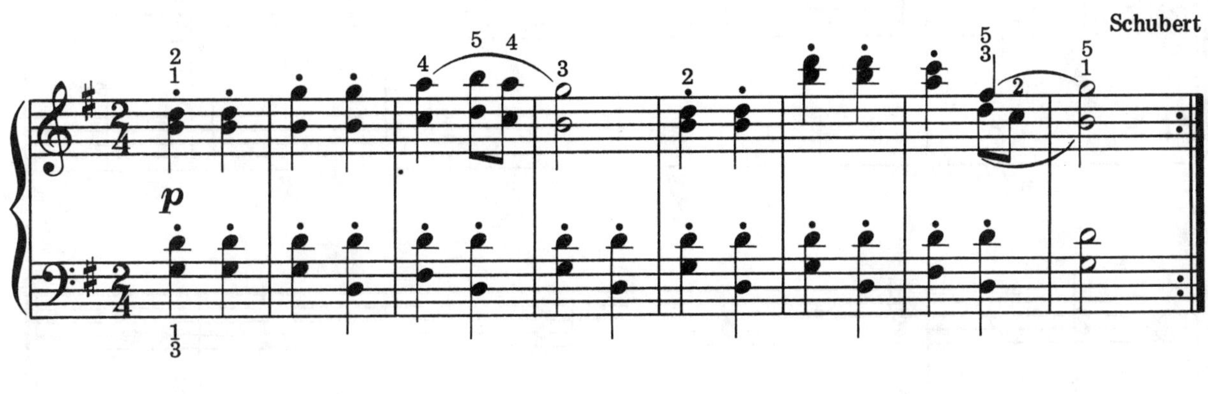

7. PRAYER

Adagio

Cornelius Gurlitt

8. AMERICA

Henry Carey

Selections 8-13 (pp. 250-53) from *The Golden Book of Favorite Songs.* Copyright 1946 by Hall and McCreary; copyright renewed 1974 by Schmitt, Hall & McCreary. Used by permission.

9. SOFTLY NOW THE LIGHT OF DAY

10. INTEGER VITAE

Friedrich F. Flemming

11. 'TIS SPRINGTIME

Süssmayer

12. THE PATRIOTS

Thüringian Folk Song

13. MY FAITH LOOKS UP TO THEE

Lowell Mason

1. MARCH

From *Notebook for Anna Magdalene Bach*

2. ARIA

Domenico Scarlatti

3. ARIETTA CON VARIAZIONI

Variation I
20
25
cresc.
30

4. PRELUDE, OP. 28, NO. 4

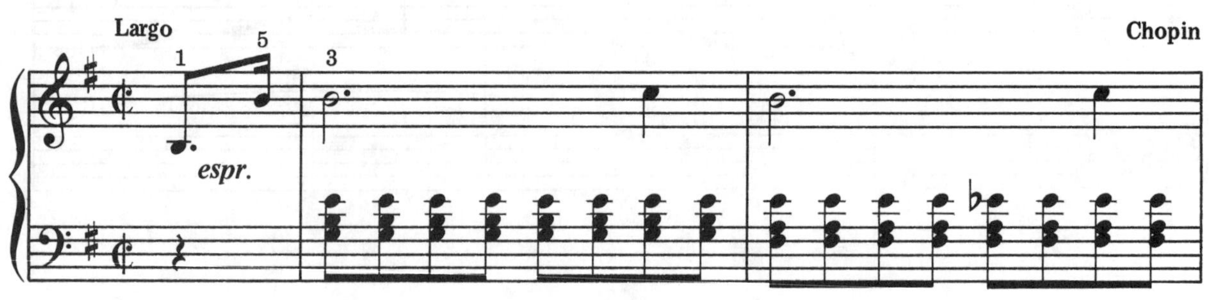

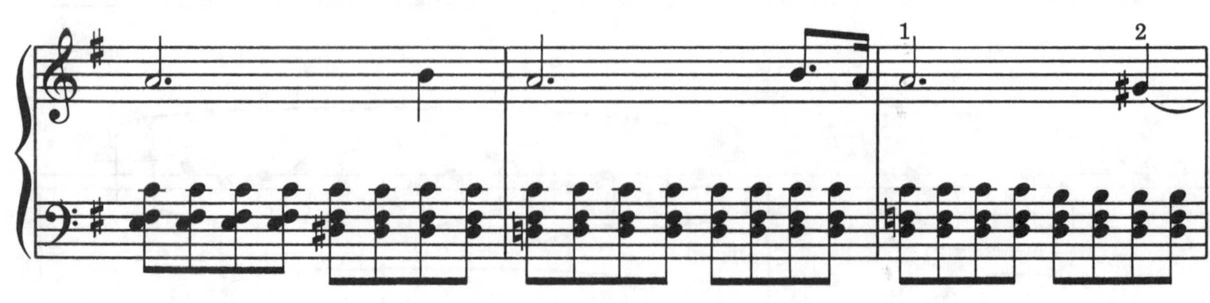

2 1 2
3
p

15
1 2
f

4
3
dim.
p
20

smorz.
pp
25

5. GLORIA

Allegro risoluto

Persichetti

From *Little Piano Book*. © Copyright 1954 Elkan-Vogel, Inc. Used by permission.

Index of Titles and Composers

Topical Index

A 9
B 0
C 1
D 2
E 3
F 4
G 5
H 6
I 7
J 8